CW01574407

LEVEL FIELD

DEZMON ROBERTSON

LEVEL FIELD

Personal Finance Made Simple

WRITTEN ON BEHALF OF COLLAR FINANCIAL GROUP

PALMETTO
PUBLISHING

Charleston, SC

www.PalmettoPublishing.com

Level Field:

Personal Finance Made Simple

First Edition

Paperback ISBN: 978-1-63837-289-9
eBook ISBN: 978-1-68515-756-2

Table of Contents

"Dishonest money dwindles away,
but whoever gathers money little by little makes it grow."

—Proverbs 13:11

"One in four parents reported that they never or almost never talk to their kids about household finances."
—Guidant

"As of August 2020, 21% of U.S. adults had no emergency savings."
—Bankrate

"In 2019, total auto debt in the U.S. was $1.3 trillion, increasing $59 billion since 2018."
—Debt.org

"Approximately 202,000 consumers had a bankruptcy notation added to their credit reports in the fourth quarter of 2019, an increase from the 195,000 in Q4 2018."
—Federal Reserve Bank of New York

"From 2015 to 2019, Americans' consumer credit card balances have nearly doubled, growing from $72 billion to $143 billion."
—TransUnion

"54% of student loan holders didn't attempt to figure out their future monthly payments before taking out their loans."
—GFLEC

"66% of millennials don't feel on track when it comes to saving for retirement, mostly due to the burden of housing costs."
—TD Ameritrade

"40 Financial Statistics for 2021." *Intuit Mint Life* (blog). Intuit, June 11, 2021. https://mint.intuit.com/blog/financial-literacy/financial-statistics/.

______________________'s

Financial Transformation Journey

Your Step-by-Step Checklist

- ❑ **Know your why**
    - ○ Set goals for yourself that will promote your success
    - ○ Find your motivation
    - ○ Build your support system with an accountability partner
- ❑ **Know where your money is going**
    - ○ Develop a budget that accounts for every dollar
    - ○ Spend intentionally using a budget and your spending-plan goals
    - ○ Create a net worth tracker
- ❑ **Build your basic savings**
    - ○ Build enough savings to cover deductibles, or have at least $1,000
- ❑ **Review your protections**
    - ○ Look over insurance policies to ensure adequate protection and efficiency
    - ○ Establish a freeze to protect your credit
    - ○ Review life insurance policies to ensure your family's coverage
- ❑ **Initiate Retirement Savings**
    - ○ Take full advantage of your employer match
    - ○ Review your current investments and research your available options
- ❑ **Get Consumer Debt–Free**
    - ○ Tackle the credit card debts first, focusing on one at a time by balance; move from smallest to largest while practicing lifestyle deflation to accelerate the process
    - ○ Move on to all other consumer debts, one at a time from the smallest to largest balance

- ❑ **Develop Your Full Savings**
    - Build your foundation of three to six months of necessary expenses
- ❑ **Focus On Retirement Preparation**
    - Dedicate at least 15 percent of your income to retirement savings
    - Develop an investment plan that will meet your needs for retirement
- ❑ **Build Your Legacy Plan**
    - Think about the financial legacy you wish to leave
    - Establish and update beneficiaries for all your accounts periodically
    - Get your wills and/or trusts in order to accomplish your wishes
- ❑ **Make allocations for your money**
    - Make allocations to enjoy, invest, save, and be charitable with your money
    - Seek professional help to further develop your investment and tax strategies for your wealth

Introduction

Right now, about 65 percent of Americans are living paycheck to paycheck. We're living with a mortgage and one to two cars purchased with debt. We have credit card debt averaging around $6,000. There are student loans, lingering debt from medical bills, and miscellaneous personal debts eating away at our paychecks every month. We work at our jobs out of the need to pay our bills and debts, not because we truly feel fulfilled in our craft. If there is anything left after our payments, we find that it somehow manages to escape our bank account without our being intentional in how it was spent. We fall prey to this cycle of working to make more money to keep up with debt that continues to run away from us. This is the typical story we grew up with and are now experiencing in our own financial lives.

The good news is that this doesn't have to be your story, but it is a tough road ahead to begin building better money habits. This book provides the help needed, walking you step by step through the process of eliminating the inefficiencies in your financial life, which will lead you to breaking this cycle and building wealth for yourself. As you begin to understand how money works and learn to view it as a tool, you will see that making purposeful financial decisions naturally follows. Your future will start to fill with confidence, and you will have a more secure outlook for what's in store.

Personal finance should be taught to all of us in school to best set us up for success in adulthood. It is a true tragedy that in most cases it doesn't make the curriculum. Our money habits are then learned through trial and error and our own observations of others. Those of us that don't have examples of good financial habits may never learn the keys to success in this field. This inequity in one of the most important aspects of our livelihood proves the need for a common foundation of knowledge across all people. It leads to the two main goals for this book: First, it will provide this knowledge to level the playing field for those left behind on the educational side of handling their money. Second, it will push those who already excel in their personal finance habits to review their complete financial plan, ensuring it provides the stability, protection, and efficiency to fit their goals and lifestyle.

Here's a fun fact: one of the most common jobs of self-made millionaires is teacher. You may ask yourself how that is possible when teachers are known to be underpaid. The answer is that a teacher, on a teacher's average salary, is more than capable of becoming a millionaire when they are disciplined and smart with their finances. Being a teacher is synonymous with discipline because teachers teach it every day of their careers. The statistic proves that the concept spills over to their financial lives and is more important than the advantage that other higher-salary professions may have. Teachers practice enough discipline to save, invest, and pay down debt over the long haul until they ultimately reach that millionaire milestone. This fact should be encouraging for those that think their income puts them out of reach of building any kind of wealth for themselves.

Imagine a world where you don't have a car payment, student loans, credit card debt, personal loans, or any other kind of consumer debt to make payments on every month. Your money goes toward building upon your sum of assets making up your net worth. You live in a house and drive cars that fit comfortably into your financial picture. Your income feels like it's yours because you own your lifestyle.

In this world, you are in a position where you could do more of what you want, when you want to do it, and however you want. There is no one to tell you how you can and can't spend your money because you don't owe it to anyone else. There is nothing to hold you back from chasing your dreams. You don't have to work a job that you don't like just to make ends meet. If you do, you can feel free to quit and find something closer to your passion. It wouldn't even faze you to make these decisions. You may decide to take a year off work to recuperate before changing career fields. You may decide to begin working a new career cycle where you regularly take a planned hiatus to spend time enjoying your most youthful years. You may decide it's time to stop working altogether and retire early. You may decide to start a business that will drive your true passion. The point is that you have a never-ending list of possibilities, and you can give yourself the power to make these decisions. This is the life of a financially independent and financially free person.

All these things are possible. Really feel the words as you read that last sentence. It's simple but not easy by any means. It's a wonder more people don't strive for this level of freedom. They either haven't been taught how or aren't disciplined enough to accomplish this. It takes years, sometimes decades, of discipline and motivation to get there, but it's absolutely possible for anyone. When you do make it there, you'll see that the journey was long and full of sacrifices; however, you'll agree the payoff is so much more than worth it.

This is the journey that we will walk through in this book. We'll break down a lot of the different parts and steps that you will have to take. The disclaimer is that everyone's situation is different and unique to them. This means that in this book we can't possibly answer every question for every situation, but the general information is here. Any unique questions or needs that you have outside of this can be answered by meeting with a financial professional.

There will be bumps in the road as things come up and attempt to slow you down. People may call you crazy for setting such high goals for yourself. Others may be jealous and try to discourage you. Your motivating factor may begin to fade. There are an unlimited number of ways that you can be challenged. This is why so few succeed. However, we know there will be difficulties, and we will prepare ahead of time to succeed regardless.

To be best prepared, you will need to find or build a support system. This will be someone or something that motivates you in the toughest moments. Choose what you know will keep that fire inside you burning bright as you progress. It needs to be motivating enough to convince you to stay the course through whatever difficulties cross your path. Whether it is the goal of being able to afford something that you couldn't before or whether there is someone that you want to create a better life for, it needs to be your most effective motive. I highly recommend that your support be a spouse, close friend, sibling, parent, or another family member who is tied to you in a way that makes them truly invested in your success. If you have a spouse, the most efficient way to meet any goals will be to unite your finances and work together as your money combines to support your agreed upon goals.

Remember through the tough times to look to your support system. This is the reason that we focus on building this from the beginning. Talk to that person that you are working toward building a better life for. Drive through the neighborhood where you want to be able to afford to live one day. Dream of the business that you want to prepare yourself to be able to start. Let that motivating support system be just that when you need to re-fuel your fire. Always take the time to look at the progress that you've made, and realize that progress grows exponentially as you keep going further.

Packing List

Let's begin. Here is the packing list for what you'll need:

1) Find your motivation.
2) Find your goal.
3) Get that fire inside of you ignited.
4) Find your support system and accountability partner(s) for the journey.
5) Open your mind to learning new things, and we will take care of the education piece.

We're excited to see the success stories from those who go through this. The first part of any journey is ensuring that you prepare yourself, so pack adequately for it according to the list and follow along in the checklist as you read and take action in your life. Let's do this!

PART 1: REALIZATION

Part one is all about developing the plan for how you're going to better your financial life. Every construction project starts with a blueprint. So does every great financial plan. Here we'll walk through setting goals, tracking where your money is going, and learning how to redirect your money to where you need it to get you to your goals. These are all actions that should be taken initially to ensure you are providing yourself the best opportunity to be successful on this journey.

Goal Setting

The very first step will be goal setting, which is of key importance when it comes to getting your financial health together. Your goal gives you something to move toward. We stated earlier that this is a long journey, so you need goals to help you stay the course and keep motivated along the way. Goals also give you a way to measure where you are against where you want to be. They help you visualize your progression, which also plays into keeping your motivation high.

Goal setting sounds easy because we constantly develop goals without giving it much thought. When it comes to finances, goal setting can get a little bit more complex because it is such a long-term game. Your goals will morph along the way as life events happen to you or your family. This means that your goal sheet will be more of a working document than a concrete declaration. There are some general rules you should follow to develop strategic financial goals that will serve as your guardrails to keep you on course and motivated.

Specific and Definitive

Rule number one: your goal has to be specific. I'll give you two examples. You should not just say, "I want to get rich." You should not simply say that you want to retire early. Those are fine aspirations, but you have to be much more specific about what your actual goal is. If you're not specific, then how do you know when you have reached your goal? Saying that you want to retire early is great, but how will you know when you are actually able to retire early? If you just say, "I want to be rich," then you haven't defined what rich is and how you'll know when you're there. Your goal needs to be specific enough to give you those guidelines. You can't practice good progression tracking without those specific guidelines set out in front of you.

Let's give an example of what a goal should sound like. We'll morph "I want to be rich" into a goal that is more specific. Let's instead try saying, "I want to have a net worth of $1 million." Instead of saying, "I want to retire early," let's try saying, "I want to have $500,000 in my retirement portfolio and the house and car paid off before an age fifty-five retirement." Those goals give you specific objectives to meet. They're definitive enough for you to be able to see exactly when you have reached your goals.

Measurable

The second part of the goal-setting exercise is to make sure your goals are measurable, which means they need to be something you can track as you progress toward your final objective. Let's take a sports example just to prove that these guidelines apply to any topic. You shouldn't say, "I want to have a good basketball season." That is another great ambition, but it's not definitively measurable. The goal should sound more like, "I want to get at least fifteen wins over the course of the twenty-five-game season." You can track your progress toward this goal by counting your wins along the journey, and you'll always know how close you are to reaching your goal for the season.

As it relates to personal finance, you wouldn't want to set your goal as "I want to be able to leave my job and go pursue my dream of writing journalism." That goal is good in that it would truly bring you career happiness; however, it's hard to measure your progress. How will you know how close you are to being able to leave your job and pursue your dream career?

Let's rework that goal to make it measurable: "I want to pay off my car, have all my credit card debt cleared, have six months' worth of emergency funds saved, and have my next journalism job lined up in order to leave my current job to go pursue my dream." Now you have specific criteria that you can use as a measuring tool to show when you've reached your goal. You know how close you are to paying off your debts and setting up your emergency fund. That will tell you how close you are to reaching that part of your goal of being able to leave your job and pursue journalism. When it comes to having your next journalism job lined up, you can set up interviews and get a start date for that job after meeting your other criteria. This goal is now measurable, and you can keep tabs on your progress.

In the times when your goals seem hard to meet, you will be able to go back and use the definitive progress you've made thus far to motivate you to not let that progress go to waste. This aspect of goal setting is important because you are setting yourself up now to be prepared to succeed through the toughest moments of the journey. What better way is there to ensure success than to prepare for the best and worst of times?

Realistic

Your goals have to be realistic, which can mean very different things to different people. It's tricky because things are more realistic for some people but less for others. When it comes to ensuring reality, let's talk about the fine line between ambitious and unrealistic.

You may want to say, "I will build a $1 million net worth by the time I reach my retirement age. I am thirty years old now, so that gives me a long range of income-making years to build toward that goal." The average American household makes right around $55,000 per year. If you make that income, you will not realistically want to set a goal of reaching $1,000,000 in just ten years for a young retirement. That would not be attainable without having a realistic game plan to get there. While it is possible to win the lottery for $1,000,000 at some point, you could not consider the lottery your realistic game plan. However, if you have a business plan in an industry that you have studied and can bring value to, then it may be realistic for you to start a million-dollar business in that timeframe. The point is to ensure that your game plan is realistic to get to the ambitious goals you want to set for yourself.

Go ahead and set ambitious goals to push you to achievements you would not have accomplished otherwise. Just make sure you use real data and numbers to ensure they are reasonably attainable for you. Setting wildly ambitious goals may have you realizing defeat as soon as reality begins to set in. This is why we use quantitative data to guard against crossing the line from ambitious to unrealistic.

When you set ambitious, attainable goals, you may run into difficulty; however, you know in the back of your mind that you can achieve them because the data is there to back you up. That will keep you motivated. This also applies when, right at the very height of your discouragement, other people tell you that you can't accomplish a goal you set. Knowing it's attainable for you in your situation means that you can use that lack of belief from others to push yourself even harder.

We set goals to keep ourselves on a path to success. While we have to account for difficulty and possible failures, we also will encounter success. This means that our goals should have some changes as we see our results come along the journey. Both failures and successes will lead to shifts in timelines. If we find early success, we can be more ambitious and continue to build upon the momentum. The point is that it's important to continuously revisit the drawing board of our goals to ensure we stay in tune with keeping them ambitious and realistic.

Time Limit

The fourth part of goal setting is that your goals need to have a time limit. Let's relate this to something we have all experienced. We have all gotten a work assignment in school that we put off until the very last minute. It could be as simple as writing a one-page paper that you had known about all semester. That would be a whole four months to write this assignment. It is just about guaranteed that almost no one in the class finished it until the last month at best. Out of all the people that waited until the last month, the likely case is that none of them completed the paper until the very last week that it was due. Out of this pool of people, you could bet that at least half of them, due to their procrastination, stayed up late on the last night to finish the assignment.

We naturally take up the entire amount of time that we're given to accomplish a certain task, assignment, or goal. If we tell ourselves only that we are going to do laundry or clean the house at some point over the weekend, we will go out for fun, watch TV all day, hang out with friends, or anything else we wish to do before we get to that unpleasant task we promised ourselves we'd do. We will finally either be forced to do it late Sunday night before bed or just never do it. What that means for us is that goal setting has to be bound to a time limit. We can't just say that we want to be rich. We have to add a time limit to it. We should say that we want to accomplish that goal by the time we're sixty; however, that is so long term that there need to be shorter milestones, with time limits on each.

We even want to make our short-term goals time bound. We can't just say, "I want to pay off all my credit cards." If we do that, statistics show that we will just sit on our credit card debt and wait while we push it back month after month. What we need to say is, "I want to pay off all my credit card debt within eighteen months." That ties a deadline to it. It forces us to start working now because we eliminate any excuse to procrastinate. That feeling you get when you know you have to start working now to meet your deadline is already present from the start. That's the feeling that you want to immediately start off with to capture your initial motivation from when you were first excited about wanting to accomplish whatever the goal is.

Setting specific, measurable, realistic, and time-bound goals is directly tied to your rate of success at accomplishing them. This is something that has been used for goal setting for years. It works. It forces you to set goals that will keep you motivated. Tying all of these aspects into your goals will propel you into accomplishing whatever it is that you want to accomplish.

Here's how it would sound to tie all of these principles together to set goals. Let's say our main desire is to be financially independent so we can spend more time with our family. The way we could set that goal is to first make it more definitive by breaking it down into smaller goals.

In order to be financially independent and spend more time with family, we will have to first build our estate. Let's say we define a ready estate to have at least $1,500,000 and no debts by the time we are fifty-seven years old.

Next, we need to break that down into simplified steps toward each part of our goal. In order to be debt-free, we will pay off all $6,500 in credit card debt within twenty-four months. That means that we will have to pay off at least $271 each month. This will take care of the credit card debt within the timeline. We determine that we will pay off our car note within the next eighteen months by paying at least an extra $250 each month in car payments as well. The goal to get debt-free is now ready for implementation.

Next, we set the goals for how we'll build our estate. Let's say we will save $500 per month into our individual retirement account (IRA) for the next seventeen of our working years to build our nest egg. We will also contribute to our 401(k) to get the full employer match for each of those years. Let's say we have done the math to determine by real data that this should get us to our estate goals by age fifty-seven. This aspect is now also ready for implementation.

All those little goals put together will make us reach our ultimate goal of retiring early to get the opportunity to spend more time with family. These goals are specific; we know exactly what we need to do to get there. They are measurable; we can track our progress all along the way toward accomplishing them. They are attainable; we have checked our budget and know that we can afford to meet those savings and investment amounts. Lastly, they are time bound; each of those goals has a timeline of when we want to accomplish it. This is a goal that will encourage us to get started by turning our rush of motivation at the time of setting the goal into immediate, directed actions. It will keep us motivated by setting the measuring stick for us to look back on in our times of discouragement. Overall, setting our goals in this manner profoundly increases our chances of success.

Hold Yourself Accountable

After you have done this exercise and have good, solid goals created, you need to set those goals in writing. What that means is that they need to be written down where you can see them whenever you need to reignite that motivation. The location can be in a box or drawer that you can open up to see what you have written down. You don't want to have a goal just in the back of your mind. You will subconsciously start changing that goal to make it easier on yourself by lowering your standard when you are discouraged. If you set that goal in writing, your brain automatically tells you that you're going to do it. You will subconsciously think things like, "I said I was going to do that. That is what I'm going to do." It doesn't give you an opportunity to go back and change that goal as easily.

You want to post some type of reminder of your goals where you will be forced to see it on a regular basis. If it's a picture of something that relates to your goal, you can post it on your fridge or headboard in your bedroom. You could write a personal reminder and stick it on your mirror in your bathroom or post it anywhere you will be forced to see it regularly to remind yourself that this is the goal you set and are going to accomplish. You will want to give yourself positive affirmations whenever you see it by reminding yourself of your reason why you want to accomplish it and telling yourself that you can do it. That affirmation is really powerful when it comes to keeping your confidence and motivation high.

If you want to make this exercise even more powerful, you can tell someone else what your goals are. Give your accountability partner the specifics to help them best hold you accountable. Tell them what you need to do month by month and year by year in order to reach that goal. Give them the entire playbook. That will give you someone who can follow up with you on specifics and say, "Hey, did you actually save that $500 per month? Did you actually pay that $250 toward your car note? Did you actually pay that $271 onto your credit card bill?" If you have not done it, that person will remind you and encourage you to meet those steps that you set forth.

It will also give you a little sense of embarrassment when you fail to meet your mark due to laziness or lack of motivation. There will be times when you fail and have to tell that person when they ask. It will hurt emotionally; however, having someone to hold you accountable will prevent you from just giving up right then in that moment. They will be your source of firm accountability and loyal encouragement.

Take action right now to set your goals according to these guidelines. Put them in writing and post them somewhere you'll see every day to remind you of your end goal. Make sure you channel your best source of motivation and reasoning for accomplishing your goal. Go tell your accountability partner. Have them follow up with you on your goals as time goes on. Keep track of your progress, and use it as fuel for the rough moments. The last thing is to just go accomplish what you set out to accomplish. The future you will thank the present you for laying the foundation that the future you will be enjoying. Last but not least, have fun and enjoy this process throughout all of its challenges and difficulties.

Financial Awareness

You have your first tool in your personal finance tool belt; you have solid goals set. Let's develop your second tool, your budget. This will be one of your most important tools in helping you stay on course for your goals. It serves as your road map to guide your everyday habits along the way.

Imagine that you were dropped off at a random location in a random city with nothing to guide you. You were only told that you have two hours to be at a specific location. You were dropped off with twenty other people who are strangers to the city as well. You all are now standing at the drop-off point, completely lost. But you do have one single goal that you need to meet: get to the location you were given on time.

You are standing there not knowing how to get started or which direction to begin traveling. This is a lot of us when it comes to personal finance. We find ourselves dropped in whatever position we are in financially with great intentions of achieving financial success. Even when we try to set goals for ourselves, we still feel lost about which direction to go to begin achieving what we want. We are all working toward the goal of balancing living now and financially preparing for the near and far future.

Let's go back to the scenario. How would you first go about getting to the location? You don't have a GPS, and you don't have a map. You could walk around the city aimlessly and hope that you luckily stumble upon the location; it's highly unlikely that you would ever make it there within the time constraint. This would be the equivalent of your just trying to go through your life with no financial plans or direction, hoping to eventually stumble upon financial success. In the random city, you would have to accidentally get lucky enough to walk in the very direction of the meeting location and not get distracted by any of the grand city sights and lights along the way. You would have to pass by the carnival, beachfront, and street shows with tunnel vision. All these things would just slow you down in the same way that all the advertisements of new cars, vacations, clothes, shoes, toys—all the things that we as a society love to buy when we truly aren't in a financial position for them to be wise choices—also slow us down in reaching our goals.

Careful Who You Ask

One thing you could do to help you get to the destination is asking around for directions. You have plenty of options for people to ask. Would you ask one of those strangers dropped off with you? It would not be a wise choice because they are going into this just as blind as you are. Surely you could ask them, and surely some of them would give you directions based on their best guesses; they would likely be steering you wrong.

This is the equivalent of asking for help with your finances from other people that are just as lost as you. You should ask for advice from people who have wisdom through experience or knowledge through study. In this scenario a great place to start asking for directions would be from one of the local residents. They are most likely to be knowledgeable of the area and could probably guide you to the general location, at the least. You could stop at a gas station or store to talk to someone who works there and be pretty sure they know the area much better than you do because they have the credential of living nearby.

This is the equivalent of finding someone you know who has handled their money well and asking for their guidance and advice rather than asking your other friends in the same position as you. The source of the information that you take for action needs to be well screened before you act on the advice. The absolute best person to ask for directions would be someone who is an expert in the area.

In our scenario you may seek out a cab driver who goes all over the city on a regular basis. You know pretty well that they can provide directions for you with almost pinpoint accuracy. Their advice could have you well on your way toward meeting your deadline. In this same sense, in your own life, you can consult a financial professional to ensure you're getting a great combination of academic knowledge and experience in the field.

When that cab driver gives you turn-by-turn directions, landmarks to mark your turns, and even traffic patterns to look out for, you will most definitely need to write those steps out. If you had a map, you would make note of the directions to lay out your specific route. That would be your guiding document to show you exactly how to get there. There are a ton of different routes that could get you there, but now you have the best path for you from your starting location. You can even customize it along the way. You can choose to avoid tolls, highways, known traffic stops, and so on.

Now you are getting to where you want to be in the most confident and efficient manner.

This is what a budget is for your financial journey to success. Building a budget is like building your road map or putting your location into a GPS. You design it to accomplish your end goal, and then you allow it to guide you along that journey. The best part is that, like planning a trip, you get to customize the route. You decide how loose or how restrictive your budget is. This is where your power really lies.

You are a much better decision maker for yourself when you are sitting down designing your short-term budget for the month than when you are standing in the store looking at a pair of shoes you love and trying to decide whether you should buy them. Taking the time to design your budget well really moves the needle for your chance of success in those moments. You make it harder on yourself to mess up your plan when it's budgeted out prior to spending your money.

If you don't like your budget anymore, you can always change it to better fit your situation. If your budget fails, you can further develop it to make it better. It's important to understand that you maintain control the entire time. The budget is really just a tool to help you control the power that you have to use your money as you please. In this sense we should think of the budget as giving us more power over our finances rather than as something that takes away our power.

Every well-functioning business operates on a budget. Larger businesses often have an entire financial department to track every source of income and expense down to the penny. Everything they do involving money is in line with their budget and accounted for. Why would so many businesses have these budgeting practices if such practices were not key players in successful operation? Many of the larger businesses clearly have enough money to cover all their expenses and more, but they still use a budget because they know that having one to guide their decisions is the most efficient way to meet their financial goals.

Your Budget Is Your Key

In our personal lives, it is imperative that we operate on a budget. When most people think of the word "budget," they usually think of something restrictive, telling them that they can't do this or that, or that they have to put something off. For some, a budget has to start like that. For others, it can just be a simple mental note of where they are and what they want to do with their money.

In its simplest form, everyone already keeps a version of a budget for themselves. Someone who doesn't have much money knows they cannot afford a multimillion-dollar home. That person knows this because they have a mental note of how much money they have and that it's not enough for a purchase that large. By a stretch, this is a simplified form of budgeting; it just isn't effective enough to get us to financial success. A good budget gets much more specific: you know exactly how much money you bring in and exactly where it all is going to go. It can be as simple as little notes that you keep for yourself, or it can be as complex as professional accounting software on your personal computer. It is really up to you to figure out what works best for your organization and comfort level.

Getting Started

For those just getting started, a budgeting application or a computer spreadsheet will likely be the best method for you. It doesn't have to be anything fancy. You just need something you can design to gain situational awareness of how much money you have coming in and where it's going.

You can set up a simple Excel spreadsheet with an income and expense side to get started. On the income side, put in all your sources of income. For most people that will just be their full-time job. For others it may be their full-time job and a part-time job or side hobby. Anything that brings you cash on a regular basis should go on the income side. Total these and use that sum as your total income throughout this exercise.

Next, list everything you will put money toward for the next month on the expenses side. Start with your highest-priority needs before anything else. Start with your food, shelter, and transportation. Next, go through your monthly bills, such as electricity, water, and utilities. Then list your next-highest-priority items, such as your necessary insurance bills that allow you to continue to operate your vehicles. Keep going down the line of your highest-priority expenses. Once all your necessities to live and operate legally are taken care of, mark this list as your "Tier 1" priority.

The next expenses added to the list will be your debt payments and important expenses that do not fall into the Tier 1 category. These will be debts such as credit card bills, medical debts, vehicles not necessary for you to bring home your income, and so on. This may also contain bills such as your cable TV, internet, phone bill, and other bills of this nature that are rigid or under a contract with penalties for breaking. This part of the list will be separated and marked as your "Tier 2" priorities.

Before moving on, it's important to fund your saving and investing goals. The placement here is intentional. You want to fund these goals after your necessities but before the "fun" expenses. This concept will help ensure we keep our future as a priority. If you aren't debt-free yet, include your extra principal payments on your debts in this category. Those who are debt-free will have this consist of savings for retirement, kids' college, investments, and so forth.

Once your saving and investing goals are taken care of, you can move on to your "Tier 3" priorities. This is the last necessary tier, but you can develop as many tiers as you want. If you see enough of a separation between your priorities to make a new tier, then go for it. This bottom tier will normally be expenses such as some memberships, music and streaming subscriptions, and things like this that can normally be scaled down or canceled easily without penalty. This is also where your allocations for eating out, enjoyment shopping, and entertainment would fall because they are less of a priority than any other bills and necessary expenses.

The reason for the tiers is to separate where you will later go back and focus in on your budget on a monthly revisit to align it to your new month's income and expenses. It will also help zero in on where you can make your lifestyle more efficient. In this example Tier 3 contains the monthly expenses going toward living a fun and happy lifestyle. You can visit this section to focus on the smaller, habitual monthly spending that can cause you to blow out your budget. These expenses can be changed or eliminated easily and without much impact on livelihood. Tier 2 consists of a lot of debt payment and bills that are not absolutely necessary for us to live. This is where you could look to make minor, more long-term changes to help your finances. A look in this section may make you question why you make payments for a second or third vehicle that you don't have a real need or utility for. It will also show you how much money you'll save by eliminating some of these debts. Tier 1 consists of major lifestyle changes. Focusing on this section may show you that your housing expenses are too high and cause you to look into relocating to lower your expenses. Tiers 1 and 2 together also help us determine our emergency savings level needed by separating out the expenses that count toward what we have to be able to cover in an emergency. This system makes hunting for an extra few dollars in your budget to fund a new savings goal much easier by organizing your budget based on priorities and category.

We also use this system to mark where our debt principal payments, savings goals, and investing goals fall into our priorities to ensure they get funded before less prioritized items are funded. An example of this is placing all of these goals in between Tier 2 and 3 to ensure you fund your emergency savings before you give yourself extra spending money for the month. This protects your intentions in that an unexpected interruption to your income won't take away from your monthly goals before it takes away from unnecessary expenses that can be cut out with minimal long-term impact.

Variables

For those with less conventional incomes or bills, some things that you have to budget for will be a bit more complex because your expenses or incomes are variable. If you work off commissions, own your own business, or just changed jobs, for example, then you will likely fall into this category. To plan for your income and expenses, give yourself reasonable estimates for everything. Estimate on the low side of your income, to the point where it would be abnormal if you earned any less than the amount you budget for. When it comes to expenses, estimate on the high side of your bills, to the point where it would be abnormal for your bills or expenses to be any higher than the amount written down. For example, if your electricity bill fluctuates between $60 and $95 per month, then you may estimate that your electricity bill will be about $105 per month to ensure you are using a good measuring stick. If what you spend on gas fluctuates between $70 and $85 per month, then you may estimate that you will spend about $94 per month. For those having trouble developing safe estimates for specific bills, I recommend starting at a rule of budgeting 10 percent more than the highest bill amount throughout the past year. Use this practice until you can dial it into a more precise estimate. This will give you a buffer to ensure that you don't underestimate the expense. Always remember that you are the best person to give your estimates rather than solely trying to base it off of another household's budget.

Keep in mind that you have to include allocations for any expenses that are not billed to you monthly but that you know you will need money budgeted for. For example, if you know that Christmas is in three months, a vacation is coming up in two months, or you will have property taxes due in four months, you will need money budgeted for those nonmonthly expenses to prevent them from catching you off guard. Take those expenses and build them into your budget. Give a reasonable amount that you plan on allocating monthly toward each of those according to the date you will need to have that money ready to spend. Just by simply writing these things out, you are giving yourself situational awareness of what is going on in your life and will be prepared to handle these items as they come up.

Let's make sure that your expenses are not greater than your income on a monthly basis. If they are greater than your income, then you have a financial crisis that you need to be working toward solving by raising your income, lowering your expenses, or some combination of both. If your income is greater than your expenses, then you need to figure out how much you have left over to work with. This is where you will consult your goals that you have written out previously to work through how much of this should go toward your debt payments, savings goals, investing goals, charity goals, and so forth.

Always budget to allocate every dollar that you are expecting to receive in income toward an expense or goal; this is budgeting toward zero. It ensures that you are maximizing the power of each of your dollars and not letting any slide out of your control. The total of all your budgeted expenses will always be equal to your income when following this concept. The goal is to determine how much money your lifestyle requires by using your budget to track the costs of all your bills and expenses. The money that is left after these expenses will then be strategically allocated into your budget under a few different categories. For those who still have consumer debt, any income in excess of your bills and lifestyle expenses should be budgeted toward debt payments; we will get more in depth with specific steps to do this in the chapter on gaining debt freedom. For those who have already accomplished the debt-freedom milestone, this income should be allocated toward savings, investments, or any other goals that you want to meet. Your money works much more efficiently when each dollar is assigned to an expense in this fashion.

Now that everything is written out in front of you in your budget, you can easily see where you can adjust your expected expenses, lower some of your bills, or be more intentional with your spending. Your finances are now simplified and organized, getting you one step closer to reaching your financial goals. Budgeting may be complicated in the beginning because it's tough to keep track of every expense. As you build your financial awareness of where your money is going and understand how it will be allocated toward your goals, you can then set general spending categories that allow you to spend up to a specific amount without having to track each of the expenses under that category. It simplifies budgeting and makes it more fun and easily manageable from that point forward. Getting to this level of budgeting requires building a good strategy to ultimately meet your goals, and months of practicing being intentional with your money. Your efficiency is most important, so don't hesitate to ask for help or reach out to a professional to help you get set quickly with good budgeting habits.

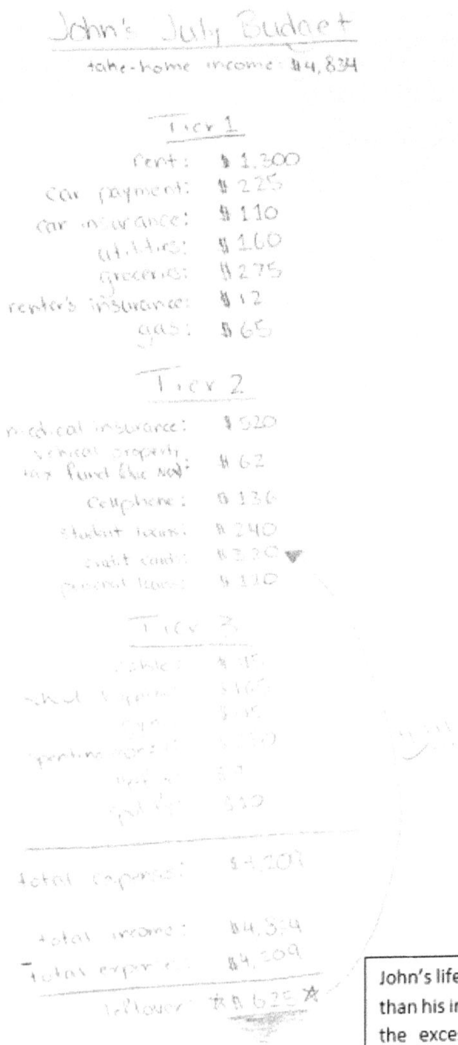

John's lifestyle costs are $625 less than his income. Here, he budgets the excess toward extra credit card payments on his journey toward debt freedom.

No Dollar Left Behind

The budgeting exercise is for your situational awareness to help you develop a plan that tells your money how it is going to work for you over the course of the period budgeted for. It will never be perfect because it's just an estimate of your income and expenses. We do our best to accurately estimate, but it will never reflect your exact reality. We can't budget too little for fear of not having enough, while budgeting too much leaves us with too many unassigned dollars that would work more efficiently when given a job to do. It's a naturally imperfect proposal. This is where constructing a spending plan will capitalize on the inherent flaws of your budget.

The spending plan is designed to assign work to any money that was budgeted but went unused at the end of the month. It ensures that not even a single dollar is allowed to wander out of your control. Let's think about what happens to the average person when they budget $90 for their electricity bill and only get billed $70. They will rejoice in the fact that their bill was low, but they lose sight of that "savings" and see it somehow gone at the end of the month. This would be a missed opportunity to use this cash. Because we estimate on the high side of every variable bill, you can see the problem with letting money sneak away from us like this across our entire budget. The spending plan capitalizes on this opportunity by assigning a job to that money. At the end of the month, you should see this sum of money as an opportunity to fund priorities. The spending plan lists out those priorities for you to go through and fund line by line.

To start your spending plan, write down how much money you need to fund your budget for the month. Remember, this number should be equal to your income when we budget toward zero. Next, write out what your priorities are for any excess cash from the budget that goes unspent. As we will begin to work the plan for getting consumer debt–free later in the journey, you will see the spending-plan priority should be debt-principal payments at first. Once you are debt-free, your priorities can be allocated to items such as investments, emergency savings, a vacation fund, holiday spending money, and so forth. Go through each priority and, on each item, write the maximum amount or percentage that you would want to fund before moving on to the next priority. Continue with this until you have accounted for any amount of money that could be unused in your budget. That is all it takes. It's as simple as that.

At the end of the month, write out the total spent on your actual expenses and subtract it from your budget. This will give you the amount of excess funds left that can now be used to fund the priorities laid out in your spending plan. Go down the line, funding each priority in the order that you laid them out, until each dollar is spent. Getting to put an extra lump sum into your vacation fund or investment account will bring a feeling of joy that will work to encourage you to stay toward the lower end of your budgeted expenses in hope of being able to fund these accounts more at the end of the month.

Your spending plan is a tool to recapture the inherent inefficiency of the overestimating built into a good budget. It makes you see this money as an opportunity to do more work rather than as "extra" for you to spend frivolously. It's a helpful thing to consult when you run into financial windfalls, such as tax refunds and want to be smart and efficient with the money. This is a great tool to help ensure you capitalize on the full potential of each dollar of your income.

Between your goals sheet, spending plan, and monthly budget, changes in each document will affect the trajectory of the others. They all work in harmony with one another to guide your financial life, so it's important to design them all well. Using this system, the end of the month would consist of funding your spending-plan priorities with the money left over from your budgeted expenses, designing the new month's budget that will account for any changes in income or expenses, and updating your goals sheet to ensure you are tracking along the path needed to accomplish your goals. You will feel like the ultimate master of your money doing these at the end of each month. Have fun with your new power over your dollars!

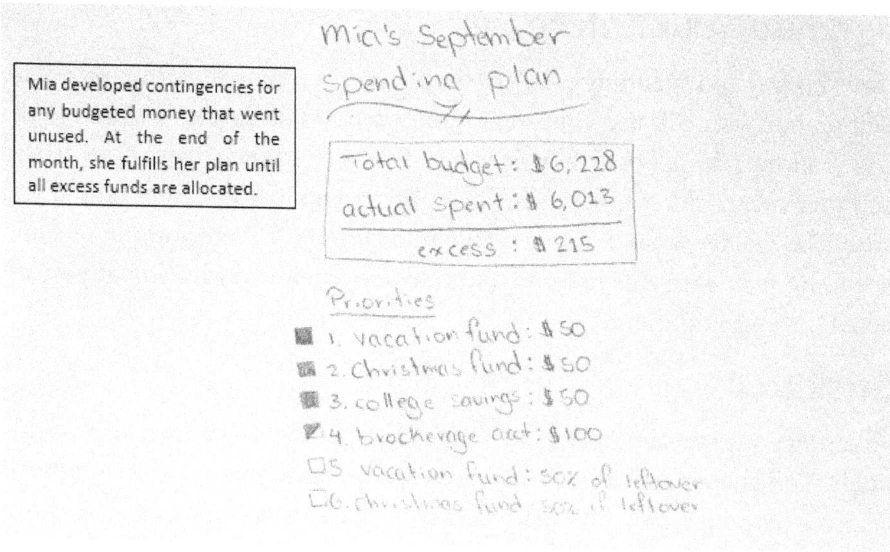

Tailored to You

Remember that this is all highly customizable to what fits your goals and your lifestyle, so you have to continue to mold this to your needs as you see fit. The tier system will be different for everyone. For example, if you work remotely from home, your internet bill is a much higher priority than it is for someone who only uses their home internet for gaming and movie streaming. As your income has minor monthly fluctuations, your budget and spending plan will adjust. The important piece is that you continue to regularly revisit your budget and spending plan. Doing this will ensure it stays accurately customized to meet your needs and intentions.

Your document or spreadsheet should be pretty full by now. Make sure you have a way to keep constantly tracking and expanding as you add and subtract expenses and savings and investing goals, whether it's working across rows or down columns. Keep track of your progress, and change your budget and spending plan as you go on. I highly recommend a spreadsheet application on your cell phone or computer to optimize flexibility for updates to your documents.

Promise Your Future Self

Your budget and spending plan are simply your agreement with your future self on how you will use your money to meet certain goals. As you're writing it all out, think about how it would hurt you to hear from your future self that you couldn't follow your plan. Just imagine how disappointed you would be to have wasted so much diligent planning. Create your budget and spending plan with this in mind and remember your motivation as you are actively designing them.

Stick to It

Creating your spending plan and budgeting comes with its own level of difficulty and challenge for everyone. Some people find that it takes months of changes to get it right. The really difficult part of it all, however, is sticking to it.

Everything may sound great on paper. You intend to spend exactly this certain amount on these categories. When you get to the end of the month, you may realize that you blew that portion of your budget out of the water. You may also find that you spent money on lower-tier items, which left you without money to fund a higher-tier item. This happens and is nothing that can't be resolved. It is inevitable that people will run into these issues. It comes with the territory of taking on this task of getting in control of your money. You are actually retraining your brain into a new way of thinking about how you fundamentally use and spend your money, so difficulties are expected.

There are tips and tricks that work for different people to resolve some of these difficulties. The goal is to find the tricks that work best for you to help you get going on the process as efficiently as possible. In this case, time is money. Therefore, we want to waste as little time as possible in getting over the initial troubles. For instance, a person that can't quite meet their budget on certain items can make small tweaks to correct this issue. A person with major trouble meeting their budget could have to go as far as only bringing with them the exact amount of cash they intend to spend in any store.

Fast and effective resolving action is what you want to achieve by nailing these issues down in the beginning. Every month that you spend trying to get started is more time and money wasted. This is where connecting with a financial coach will be an effective route to get you started on the path most efficiently.

Your money is one of your keys to a healthy and successful lifestyle, so you have to know what it's doing at all times. At this point you know how you're going to control it, and you are now telling your money what to do for you. You gain so much financial control just by simply following these steps and writing these things out into a plan. It forces you to be more conscious of your spending habits. You will now think twice about spending more on something than you budgeted for and will be less tempted at the store by things that would have previously been irresistible to purchase on a whim. You'll be maximizing every dollar with your spending plan. Your system will be a smooth, efficient machine that pours confidence and success into your financial life.

Know Your Worth

The next thing you need to create is a net worth tracker. This sheet is going to be another very powerful tool for your self-awareness and progress tracking toward your long-term goals. This net worth tracker will ultimately break down where your worth lies. In its simplest form, it's just a list of what you own and owe. This one is simply a spreadsheet broken up into two sides. On one side, you have your assets. On the other side, you have your liabilities.

On the asset side, list out everything that you own and the value that it has. Let's start with the simplest one first, your accounts of value. List your retirement accounts, such as your 401(k), IRAs, and so forth. List any other liquid accounts that you own or control, including your bank accounts—checking, savings, and any investment accounts. Next, list any equity that you have in your other assets. Continue listing anything that you have of value that can be a contribution to your worth.

The assets to avoid listing are depreciating assets. For example, do not list your vehicles, because your vehicles are typically worth less and less over time. Do not list appliances or furniture that you have, because they are worth less with each passing year as well. The only time that I recommend listing any of those depreciating assets is if you are listing them in a plan to immediately sell them for cash to pay off debt, save, or invest.

On the other side of this spreadsheet, list out all your liabilities—this is anything that you owe to someone else. For example, if your home is worth $290,000, then your asset side should show $290,000. But if that home still has a mortgage for $200,000 on it, then your liabilities side should also show $200,000. As your home's value rises, your assets side will grow. As you pay off your mortgage, your liabilities side will shrink. Continue listing your credit card debts, student debts, medical debts, and any financed items that you have. Once you have all your debts listed, tally up your assets and liabilities sides separately. Subtract your liabilities from your assets. This calculation is your net worth.

If you have a negative net worth, don't stress out too much because this is all about the realization of where you are. We will get that net worth growing in a positive direction in time. With these three items—your budget, spending plan, and net worth statement—you will form the basis of your financial records that will ensure you reach your goals.

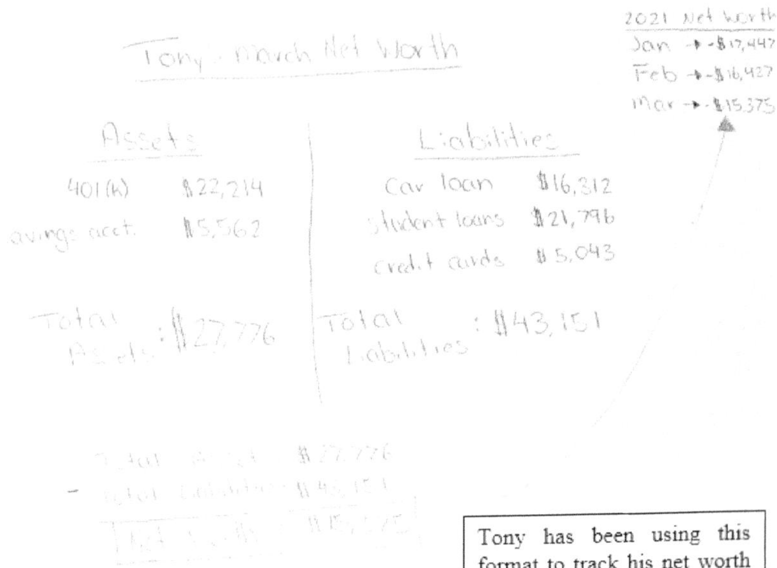

Tony has been using this format to track his net worth throughout the year. Although it is negative, you can see it's increasing as Tony focuses on getting debt free

Congratulations—you are now armed with solid goals, financial awareness, and a plan for action. Your tool belt is full of everything you need to get started on this journey. The tool belt will continue to grow and morph into what fits your particular needs as you continue to learn and grow. Having this at your disposal should already leave you feeling a deep sense of confidence that you are taking steps toward creating a brighter financial future for yourself. Keep that confidence, and build on it with results.

PART 2: GEARING UP

Part two is all about ensuring you have your bases covered to soon be ready for taking action. Let's talk about making sure your savings and protections are put into place. These are some of the fundamentals of good financial planning and should be a focal point at this stage of getting your money in order. We'll also take a glance at retirement planning to make sure we don't pass up free money while we're buttoning up the rest of our finances.

Savings: Part I

One of the most important pieces to gaining freedom and peace of mind is having adequate savings. You need to have some cash set aside that will be safe and there for you when you need it most. In other words, you need liquid cash savings that are easy to get your hands on in an emergency. You should keep your cash in either a savings account at your bank, a money market account, or some type of high-yield savings account. Anywhere your money can meet the criteria of being safe, liquid, and easily accessible in an emergency will be fine for this purpose. Cash is both your rock and your cushion that serves as your safety net and foundation of your wealth.

How Much Is Enough?

The question is always, "How much cash savings do I need?" The answer is a little complex and different for everyone. In this first part of savings, if you haven't yet gotten consumer debt free, it's a little simpler. You should have at least enough to cover the deductibles on your insurance policies. At a bare minimum, you should keep at least $1,000, even if your deductibles are less than this.

Let's say that your highest deductible stands at $1,500 for the policy on your home. You should set aside $1,500 as your savings at this step in the journey. If your highest deductible is only $500, then you should set aside $1,000. The goal is to have enough in savings to protect you in the event of an actual emergency situation while still being able to focus the maximum amount of money on getting your finances in order. It wouldn't do you much good to throw every dollar you had at debt, deplete your savings, and have to resort to taking on high-interest credit card debt to pay your insurance deductible in the event of a car accident. The purpose of ensuring we complete this savings goal at this stage is to prevent such situations. It's all about ensuring you're being both smart and efficient during the process.

Later on, in part two of savings, we'll talk about what your emergency savings should look like once you've achieved consumer debt freedom. This is where you hear the classic saying of up to six months' worth of emergency savings. Always remember there is a time and place for almost everything. In this case the time for getting the fundamentals of your emergency savings is before you begin aggressively eliminating consumer debt. The time for fully stocking your savings is after you are free from consumer debt.

Protection

Because we're protecting ourselves by ensuring that our savings can cover our insurance deductibles, it only makes sense to ensure that our insurance is actually protecting us. Life can be so unpredictable and unfortunate, and terrible things happen to people seemingly out of nowhere that put them in a financial crisis. This next exercise is going to be thinking through all of our insurance protections against some of the most common mishaps that can ruin us financially. Let's make sure that we actually have proper protections in place. After all, this is what insurance is all about.

Why It's Important

Insurance companies take the very low probability, but highly financially damaging, events that could happen in our life and pools the payments from all the policyholders together to cover the damages when the event occurs to an individual policyholder. It protects the few people that actually experience the event. On an individual scale, you are effectively paying for the peace of mind of having that risk taken off your hands for the period you're covered, even though it likely never happens to you. It becomes almost ironic that we pay on a regular basis for something that we hope to never use; however, insurance still remains a very important piece of our financial plan. It's what provides us more stability and confidence in our future. So let's talk about some common pieces of insurance and ways to think through making sure they are set up correctly for us.

Car Insurance

Let's start with car insurance. If you have a vehicle, you should have insurance on it. There are so many different insurance companies and policies to choose from that it can be head spinning trying to figure out what you need and which company to get it from. With car insurance specifically, there are some basic principles to put into place to make sure that you're getting your needs covered.

The most important thing you need is to ensure that you have adequate liability coverage to fit your lifestyle. This means that you need to verify that your liability coverage can reasonably cover the total amount of property damage that could come in the event of an accident. The state minimum coverage is usually not enough to be reasonably protected. We usually recommend following the 100/300/100 rule at a minimum to ensure you can drive around feeling confident and protected. This is $100,000 per person in injury coverage, $300,000 maximum coverage per accident, and $100,000 coverage in property damages.

Savings Lead to More Savings

When you get to the point of having adequate savings in your emergency fund, then some of the extras that an insurance company offers may not be as necessary as they have been before. For example, you may not need car rental replacement coverage if you have the cash on hand to be able to rent temporarily or replace your car. You won't need to pay for the bonus replacement value coverage if you know you have the cash to be able to handle the extra costs of buying a new car that the value of your old car may not sufficiently cover. If you do not have any cash savings, then you might want to keep some of these protections; however, having that quick-access cash pile provides an opportunity to save some money by opting out of some of the extra coverages that you can then financially support taking on the risk for yourself. Keep in mind that you still are the best deciding factor in the end for what coverages you need.

If there is a loan out on your car, it is very common for you to be required to have collision coverage by your lender. Once you own your car fully, then that collision coverage is no longer required. You may feel more comfortable with it, or you may want to drop it. This is where you get to make the decisions now. You gain the freedom to choose what fits you based on how you drive and how comfortable you are financially. This is how paying off your car can go another step in saving you big money over the years. The disclaimer here is that you don't want to just start dropping coverages simply because they aren't required anymore. You have to always consider what is applicable to your lifestyle.

Claims Are Not for Convenience

The great part about most insurance policies is that you get another portion of control in the cost of your insurance by being able to choose the deductible on your policy. I recommend operating on the higher end of the deductible scale after you have the cash on hand to be able to cover them. This is where you can really save on insurance expenses. When you have a really low deductible, you pay a lot more per month in insurance because the insurance company sees you as a higher risk for filing a claim. It may seem like the difference between having a $250 deductible and a $1,000 deductible is not a big one, but think about how much more likely a person would be to file a claim if it didn't cost them much to file it. You will be much more careful to use your insurance only when it is really necessary if it costs you more to file the claim.

It's rare that we file insurance claims on small-ticket items. Consumers are already generally aware that filing a claim will usually result in higher insurance premiums on all their policies. For this reason we usually end up paying for small inconveniences out of pocket instead of filing a claim. That very fact tells you that paying for the lowest deductible may result in a higher premium that doesn't reflect the reality of your insurance needs. This is a very interesting nuance to explore to save yourself money every month, so go ahead and raise your deductibles to show the insurance company that you are responsible enough to not abuse your policy. You'll see the impact in lower monthly payments. The big disclaimer with this is that you must ensure you have the cash savings to be able to make those deductible payments if the situation arises that you need to file a claim. If you meet this condition, then you can lower your insurance bill as much as possible by choosing the highest deductibles available.

Let's move on to home and property insurance. Again, you want your insurance to cover the big-ticket items that could ruin your financial life. For example, you want your insurance to step in if your house burns down, if you have a hurricane that completely tears your house apart, or if you have a flood that causes thousands of dollars' worth of damage. This is what insurance should be used for. It should not be used to cover small incidentals, so if you have the lowest deductibles here, raise them to represent what you need the coverage for. But I cannot stress enough that you must make sure you keep the cash savings to cover those deductibles!

Landlords Don't Protect Your Belongings

If you are a renter, your landlord is responsible for the insurance on the physical building that you live in; you, however, are usually responsible on your own for your property inside of the residence. For example, you should have renters' insurance to cover your furniture, clothes, and valuables inside the home. Ensure you have enough coverage to handle actually replacing those things. Should something happen that causes a loss of your items, you will be on the hook to replace or live without them. There are so many renters that live on the minimal amount of coverage, leaving them extremely vulnerable to a financial disaster in the event of a loss. Again, with the cash on hand, you can raise your deductible to lower your monthly premium to help offset the cost of any potential need to increase your coverage.

Life Insurance Is for Your Loved Ones

Life insurance is another major category of coverage that needs to be addressed because many people don't carry enough coverage to fulfill their families' needs. Here are a few rules for life insurance: If there is anyone who depends on your income to live, then you need life insurance. If you are married, have kids in the home, or are responsible for the care of anyone, then you should have life insurance to replace your income in the event that you aren't present to provide that care anymore.

As a general rule, you should plan for at least ten times your annual income in life insurance. This is a very generic version of a rule to help give you an idea where to start, so there are cases where someone may need more or less. Let's give you some things to think about. Imagine you are a married individual and the sole provider for your household; your spouse is 100 percent dependent on your income. If your spouse is more than capable of getting back into the workforce, then you may not need the full amount of insurance recommended. But if your spouse would be incapable of bringing in any income, you may need much more than the recommended insurance level.

There are many factors that determine the amount of life insurance you should have. At a bare minimum, you want to carry enough insurance for your dependents to be able to pay off all your debts and have the time to adjust to living without your income. That rule leaves a large margin for your discernment, but you can always consult a professional for help determining how much insurance coverage you should include in your financial plan.

There are different types of life insurance policies—term and permanent policies. If you are using this book because you are getting started getting out of debt, then a term policy is likely right for you. Simply ensure that you get a level-term policy, which means that your premium will be fixed for the entire length of the policy's coverage. This will keep your financial planning simple and predictable. As your life goes on and you renew your insurance policy, you will see the premium increase. This is because aging means that you have a higher chance of passing during that next term. It's the unfortunate truth of the life insurance business. The goal, however, is to get you to a point where you will need very little life insurance.

Permanent insurance policies can be great for individuals who are already financially well off and looking for a complementary solution to long-term planning and legacy building. So stick with the term policy for now if this doesn't describe your situation. A permanent policy could possibly be a fit for your goals later down the road, when long-term planning and legacy building become your main focus.

Once you are so financially independent that you don't need much insurance, then you may be able to get a really cheap policy or drop it altogether. You can consider yourself self-insured because all final expenses can easily be taken care of from your estate, and any dependents that you have can be adequately supported. At this point it may be okay to let your policy expire at the end of the term and take it as an opportunity to lower your monthly expenses in retirement.

Big Picture

The ultimate goal here is to make sure that you have a proper insurance planning aspect in your financial plan. You work so hard to get you and your loved ones to where you are that you should take the time to ensure you don't lose your wealth due to a lack of insurance planning. The goal is to never need it, but proper insurance planning and coverage provides you with some peace of mind if things go wrong.

The things we insure are very low probability, so it's easy for us to not take insurance seriously. It really only becomes serious when that low-probability but highly damaging event actually happens to us. So let's ensure you are as fully prepared as possible now. Take the time to make sure you set your coverage plans properly with realistic deductibles so that you are adequately protected against risks in a cost-efficient manner.

Having a good foundation of savings or proper insurance protections can provide great feelings of security and stability in your life. Having them both together in an all-encompassing financial plan, however, gives you so much faith and comfort in your future that you can't put a price tag on what it's worth.

Credit Protection

Credit scores have become a focal point of our financial lives. Most people think of how their scores determine how much money they can borrow and at what interest rate; however, they affect much more than that. It can also affect your odds of approval for renting an apartment, your insurance rates, your ability to open utility accounts, and more. Even for those who are debt-free and plan never to use lines of credit again, your credit scores can still be used by companies to tell what kind of customer you are. It may not always be the fairest determinant of a person's character, but it's important that we understand its importance in the financial world and learn to protect it.

One easy way to protect your credit is to do a credit freeze. It's free, it's simple, and it takes only a few minutes to set up. Placing a freeze on your credit tells the credit bureaus that you don't want any company to be able to view your scores. The only way a company would be able to see them is for you to undo the freeze temporarily while they pull your credit information. This process is also free and simple, and it takes only a few minutes to do as well. You will find that a freeze can be an easy piece of protection to work around when it comes time for you, and only you, to use your credit when you need it.

Time and time again, we hear of identity theft being a threat to our financial well-being. Criminals are out there just waiting to get their hands on our personal information to gain access to our money, open fraudulent accounts, make purchases in our name, and so on. With a freeze in place, a criminal would have a very difficult time opening new accounts, even if they already have our personal information. We have to take steps toward identity theft prevention during financial planning because it affects our financial future. A credit freeze is a great way we can get that protection started now.

Retirement Planning Incentives

Retirement planning is a beast whose complexity has been the cause of many headaches. Most of us have an employer 401(k) that we truly don't give enough attention to, yet is one of the most beneficial and underappreciated tools available for our financial futures. We need to understand the basics of retirement planning to ensure we are taking advantage of key incentives and benefits that can be the difference maker in our ability to have a successful retirement.

Don't Pass Up Free Money

One of the benefits that we will dig into here is the employer match. It is your employer offering you free money on the condition that you save in your retirement account. A common example is an equal-percentage match up to 5 percent of your income. This means that every dollar the employee saves in retirement will be matched by the employer until it caps at 5 percent of their total income. Let's take a person making the average income of $55,000 per year who has this match available. If they were to save 5 percent of their income, that would be $2,750 per year. The employer would also be contributing another $2,750 per year on top of this. Had the person not known and taken advantage of the match, they would be passing up this great opportunity for free money from their employer. Most of us would not be happy to pass up free money. So it's important that you work to understand how your matching contributions work for your specific plan and ensure you are taking full advantage of this opportunity.

Learn Your Options

Another key factor is how your money is invested in your employer-sponsored plan. This step is not necessarily the time to make drastic moves as soon as you discover where your money has been all along. It's most important that you are taking full advantage of the match for now and getting the money in the account. As we progress through getting debt-free and buttoning up your financial life, it's a great time to also start learning about your account's options to be ready to make wise investment decisions later on once you feel comfortable in your knowledge.

Once you have your foundational savings in place, insurance protections checked, credit freeze done, and you are taking full advantage of your retirement contribution match, you are ready to move on to taking actions toward the consumer debt–freedom milestone. These steps all serve the purpose of getting your foundation set and ready for this next trek through eliminating consumer debt, so ensure you follow the steps as laid out to make sure you're prepared.

As good stewards of our communities, we should look to spread this information around and encourage others to take these actions to prepare and protect themselves. It is an easy way to spread awareness and help others who have yet to have the opportunity to learn some of this pertinent information.

PART 3: DIVING INTO ACTION

With your packing list items fully stocked, your goal sheet and financial documents in your tool belt, and preparations from Part 2 complete, you can be confident that you're ready to move right into this next section. Part 3 is all about taking action on your blueprint to financial success, which consists of multiple steps all working in harmony to efficiently get you toward the success you wish to reach. The main goal of this part is to get debt-free with a ready fund of savings put in place to provide peace of mind and stability to your life. This can take years for some people, so it's important to maximize efficiency through a consistent drive for improvement by constantly educating yourself and building a habit of seeking guidance when needed.

Debt Freedom

It's time to tackle what will likely be your biggest financial hurdle. We're going to look at eliminating bad debts. Reach into your tool belt and pull out your list of liabilities from your net worth tracker; we'll take a look at every item listed there. In this exercise we will be reviewing everything that you currently owe to someone else to see how we can clean up this portion of your finances.

Crippling Debt versus Working Debt

We are going to separate these debts into what we'll refer to as "working debts" and "crippling debts." Working debts are those that you have on appreciating assets. Usually, the only thing that you have in this category is your home mortgage. Your crippling-debt category will be things such as credit card debt, car loans, student debt, medical bills, and personal loans. These usually are the debts that have the highest interest rates. If you can get those wiped away from your life, it will propel you forward financially.

We already know how much you pay on each debt each month based on your budget. Now we are going to look at how much money you have left to be able to accelerate the payoff dates on your crippling debts first. This will save massive amounts in interest costs, which you will then be able to use to build your wealth.

Credit Cards

We have to start by putting an order to your debts. For the average person, the very first debt that you should pay off is your credit card debt because the interest rate is usually sky high in comparison to your other debts. There may be some exceptions to this rule, but for our purposes, let's start with the credit cards.

The very first thing is to *stop using them.* You may have used them out of convenience or to build points or cash rewards, but if you are carrying a balance on your credit cards, it means you have been using them wrong. Credit card balances should be paid off in full by the end of every statement period. Stop using them until you can follow this practice and get your spending habits with these cards under control. If need be, don't even take your credit card with you when you leave the house anymore. Leave it at home in the bottom of your drawer, or even go as far as asking someone you trust to hide your cards from you. The point is that you will not touch credit cards again until you can get your spending habits under control and learn how to use them.

Pay It Down

This next part is difficult, although the steps are simple. It goes against the money habits we've spent years building, so let's take it step by step to make fighting any misled inclinations we may have about debt as seamless as possible. The first step is to begin using any income you have in excess of your necessary expenses toward extra payments on your credit card balance while also only making minimum payments on any other debts so that you can focus on this one first. If you have more than one credit card balance to pay off, start with the lowest one first and continue to eliminate them in this order until you have no more credit card debt. The rest of your other debts will be paid in this same order, but only after you have finished taking care of all credit cards first—more on this later!

Write out how long it is going to take you to pay off this credit card by figuring out the maximum you can pay each month and dividing the card balance by that total amount. This is going to be an estimate of how many months it will take to pay it off, and it will help give you a target payoff date. This timeline is just your starting point as we work to improve upon your efficiency.

Think about this: credit card companies have spent millions of dollars in studies and advertisements to learn how we operate as consumers. What they learned is how to charge us a sky-high interest rate and get us to keep spending money with them. They offer us rewards and airline miles to convince us that we're beating the system and benefiting from our cards, when in reality, it actually is a way to distract us from any budget we have with a subconscious justification for using their debt for our rewards. For creditworthy customers, there can be some great perks to using credit cards; the vast majority of credit card customers, however, are used as prey by the companies to profit off the monthly carried-over balance. This means that credit card companies will keep making money as long as you have credit card debt that you carry on a monthly basis.

The credit card companies have been profiting off of us in this way for years. Now it's your turn to get back at them by not giving them any more of your money! As soon as we stop paying them, we can start paying ourselves and grow our own worth.

Challenge to You

With that being said, I challenge you to take your target payoff date for your credit card debt and beat it. Don't come up with excuses for why you can't. Don't say you have no more money to use, because you have money in your entertainment category or in some of your shopping categories. There's always spending you can cut back on in plenty of places that will seem to suddenly appear when you decide that fixing your financial life is your true priority. You can trim some of the fat off those to help speed the process of getting out of all credit card debt by accelerating how fast you pay this first card off.

Look at your expense categories, and find somewhere to help you beat your timeline. Look at everything that is not an absolute necessity to live—that is, in Tier 1—and figure out where you can trim excess fat in the other tiers. You may find that you've been overpaying for cable and that you can save by switching cable companies. Maybe you find that your car insurance is expensive and that you can save by switching providers. What you will likely find is that you spend a lot of money on unnecessary items such as drinks when you go out. Maybe you didn't realize how much money you spend on fast food and dining out. You may not have realized how much money you spend on miscellaneous expenses when you go to the store intending to get a certain item. Those will be the places where you will find easy money to help pay off debt faster. Take this challenge personally and find a way to keep beating that target payoff date!

Keep the Momentum

Once you knock out the first and subsequent credit card debts, take the money saved from those bills and apply it to your next-smallest debt. You are going to pay off all your debts in this order, from smallest to largest, while continuing only minimum payments on all other debts to focus on one at a time. There may be wise reasons to deviate from this order if you have an exceptionally high interest rate on another debt. Barring any of those anomalies, use this rule to order your medical bills, personal loans, car notes, and all other crippling debts. Go ahead and pay those off with the same intensity as you did the credit cards. The difference is that the next one will always be easier because you were able to accelerate the ones before and now have the money saved from those bills to add to your extra payments.

Doing this exercise is important because tackling these debts will put you in a much healthier financial position to be able to enjoy your money without crippling your future. By retaining all the interest money that you were previously paying on debts, you will have more income at your disposal to enjoy and build on. So let's knock out that first credit card to get the process rolling. Keep the momentum going until you eliminate all of your crippling debts. As you start paying down your debts and seeing your balances shrink, take pride in the work you are accomplishing. You will begin to feel the gratification from the journey of achieving debt freedom. Enjoy the process!

Pay Debt or Invest

There is a debate about whether your extra money is best served by paying off consumer debt or investing. I am going to encourage you to see how paying off crippling debt first will be better for you in the long run. The reason is because it is so much easier to save a dollar than it is to invest enough money to make a dollar. This means that focusing on your spending habits is the most important thing you can do to set yourself up to be a successful future investor and builder of wealth. If you focus your attention on paying down debts and making that your biggest stepping-stone, you will be more conscious of how you spend your money. You are forcing yourself to control your financial behaviors first and foremost. Controlling behavior almost always beats trying to earn your way out of bad financial decisions, such as taking on consumer debt. Also, paying off bad debt is a guaranteed result that doesn't carry the inherent risks of investment returns. With this being said, your results will be much better if you get out of crippling debts first and carry those spending habits into your lifestyle when it's time to become a strategic investor.

Personal finance is almost all behavioral. That is the hardest part of it. When you go to the store, you will think twice about buying any extra things that you don't need. It will be easier for you to say no to sales pitches. You will want to look for deals. You become a much more conscientious and wiser spender by getting the behavioral side of finance right from the beginning. This is another major reason that focusing on shedding your crippling debts first is more important than investing from the start. Once you master good money habits, your investment portfolio will build much faster and be spent more wisely.

For those that try to jump to investing before developing their spending habits, they can easily fall into the trap of thinking they are building wealth while simultaneously blowing it just as fast. You could have $1 million in assets and seem rich in the eyes of your neighbors, but it does you no good when you've racked up $2 million in debt in the process. That is how you can end up with a huge income but still live paycheck to paycheck. In fact, 20 percent of six-figure income earners are living paycheck to paycheck. Many of them worked out of order and never accomplished the basic groundwork that would allow anyone to gain financial freedom regardless of their income level. So go ahead and let bad debt be your motivation.

Once crippling debt is taken care of, you will have an even bigger amount of excess money to use to multiply the effects of investing down the road and will watch your wealth build even faster.

Stop at the Mortgage

The advice gets interesting and confusing when you are preached at to get debt-free for so long, only to get told to stop before tackling your mortgage. There is a method to the madness of why you should stop here. First and foremost, if you get this far, congratulations! You are a rock star. You have spent so much time paying off debt that you will never want to go back into crippling consumer debt ever again. You have found the secret to personal finance, controlling your financial behaviors. You are now in a position to help so many people because you are the minority when it comes to your personal finance skills. You deserve a round of applause. Now let's get back to work and keep the momentum pushing us to the next level!

The reason that we stop at the mortgage is because this is where you commonly have a really low-interest-rate loan that is so big that it will take you many years to pay off. Unless interest rates change dramatically in the future, what this means is that it's more advantageous for you to start putting all of that fire you had in paying off your other debts into setting yourself up for retirement as your primary goal before tackling the mortgage. At this point you will have already proven that your spending is under control, so this order can be much more beneficial to you in the long run. Doing it out of this order won't be detrimental to your future because you've already done well enough to put those financial worries aside forever. However, this order is just a recommendation to maximize your results.

An exception to this rule is if you are on the cusp of your last working years and getting ready for retirement. This is the time when paying off your mortgage may be the most beneficial next move to make in your retirement plan. But as a young person in your twenties, thirties, forties, and maybe even into your late fifties, this is your time to let your mortgage expense and possibly some other ultralow interest debt be secondary to your savings and investing goals. Let your primary home be an appreciation tool. If you can meet your retirement and savings goals, enjoy some of your hard-earned cash within reason, and still have money left over, then you can put that extra toward your house to pay it off faster if that is your wish.

Let's talk about setting yourself up to buy a home if this is a need that you've been trying to meet. You should be in a much better place to be able to save for a down payment to make the big purchase. It can be a daunting and confusing task to buy a first home, so we'll go through some checkpoints to keep in mind to ensure you buy one that fits your budget. Every situation is different, but you want to try to keep your expenses low while meeting your needs of comfort, safety, and happiness in your home. At a maximum, ensure you don't cross the threshold of housing consuming more than 30 percent of your income. This isn't the goal, just an absolute maximum to keep your financial health in check. Less is always best if the home still meets those goals of comfort, safety, and happiness.

Lifestyle Deflation

We've gone through how to get started on the road to achieving debt freedom, so let's talk about how to maximize efficiency on the journey. This exercise is one that will be done concurrently with debt elimination, the goal being to accelerate that process.

Lifestyle deflation is, by definition, making your current lifestyle cost less. This doesn't mean you have to give up everything that brings you pleasure in your life. It is strictly talking about taking the things that you want to keep in your life and finding ways of making them cheaper for you. This practice will help you create more money to pay down debts faster and accelerate building your portfolio to obtain the financial status that you want to have.

In this day and age of online shopping, you can almost instantly price compare just about anything with a few taps on your phone screen or keyboard. There is no reason that you should be making any splurge purchases without first shopping around to see if there is a better deal out there. Every time you decide that you need to buy a specific item, do a quick Google search to see some price comparisons first. You will likely find something cheaper than your first look at the item. You may even find something better and cheaper. Just think about how easy price shopping has become with our current access to technology. It would be sad to waste these opportunities to save money so easily.

One of the big ways to save money is by negotiating and shopping around. If you go to buy something at Target, there isn't much room for negotiation. You can, however, shop around. You can easily compare Target to every other store in your city in a matter of mere minutes while not even having to leave the store by doing the research right from your cell phone. After you compare some of the common things that you buy, you will start to get a feel for where you can look for the best deals.

A lot of times, you can look on the used market to find great deals. If you are seeking to purchase an item that isn't a consumable, then you should take a peek at the used market first. One great example of things you can find on the used market is furniture. You can save a ton of money in this category. If you ever have a need to buy any kind of furniture, it may be beneficial to start by looking at places like Facebook Marketplace and Craigslist. We live in a world where the average person moves from their home every decade or so. Many of these people decide to get new furniture during the move. Others are moving across the country and can't take all their furniture. So people are moving a lot and are essentially having giveaways on their stuff before they go. People almost never sell these items because they are broken or destroyed. It's usually something like the person is moving, they got a new one, or they just don't use it anymore. What's great about the used market is that you can get a demonstration that what you're buying is good before you buy it, and you will likely negotiate a lower than advertised price. Based on these reasons, I highly recommend the used marketplace for things such as furniture, tools, decorations, and so on.

Caution

While many experiences are great, you should be a little more wary of buying expensive electronics on the used market. The reason that I say this is because something may work on the surface, but you may find issues with it as you begin to use it. There are also a lot of scams to look out for when buying these sorts of things. If you want to go this route, I recommend looking at refurbished electronics from a certified dealer that will provide guarantees and warranties with the purchase.

Where to Begin

Common places to start deflating your lifestyle are going to be the expensive things that you can shop around for, such as your cell phone plan, your car insurance, subscriptions, and service plans. One of the easiest and most common places for people to apply lifestyle deflation is their food from the grocery store. A lot of your items can easily become better deals by simply shopping around for better pricing. There are so many competitors that companies' prices change on a regular basis in order to stay competitive. You may find promotions that are going on for some items that you commonly buy, so shop around. You have probably been using the same grocery store for years. It may be time to give another one a try.

When it comes to memberships and subscriptions, there are probably things you bought thinking that you would use them more than you actually do. Go ahead and cancel those. This will instantly free up money in your budget. Think to yourself, "Do I really need cable TV, Netflix, Hulu, Disney+, and Sling?" Which one do you use the most? How about trimming down to just those one or two of your most useful subscriptions and cutting the rest out? See how it goes for a few months. You can always sign up again for what you had. The ultimate test for items you may be indecisive about is to cancel all your subscriptions and memberships that you haven't used in the past year.

Another place to look to save money is in where you live. This is for those of you that pay excessive expenses for where you reside. So let's take a look at your primary residence. Consider moving if you are living much outside of your means and will save at least a few hundred dollars per month by relocating. Some examples of this are if you live in a really expensive apartment, bought a really expensive house, or if you live on your own but have an opportunity to share a place with a roommate. Maybe you can rent out a room where you currently live to help alleviate your mortgage or rent. There is plenty of room to get creative here and reduce your living expenses. Making leaps like this will not only accelerate your money goals but also encourage you to get your financial life in order faster after making such a lifestyle change.

Vehicle Rules

One of the biggest sources of excessive expense is our transportation. The large majority of Americans have cars that they cannot afford. Your vehicle costs should be no more than 10 percent of your take-home income. Use this as a guide to help decide whether your vehicle is within reason for your lifestyle. The vehicle payment for the average American making around

$55,000 a year and following this rule would be no more than about $325 per month to keep them in this range. Remember that this is an upper limit and not the goal you should be raising your standard to meet. You should not have a vehicle that you have to finance for more than three years. To better avoid falling underwater, or owing more in loans than the vehicle's market value, at any point during your ownership of the car, you should not be buying a vehicle with no money down. Follow these generic rules to keep your car from wrecking your financial life. The ultimate goal is to not be forced to finance your cars. Once you begin building your assets and growing your wealth, you will be able to purchase your cars in cash or choose to finance them as part of a broader plan to continue allowing your cash to grow. Your car is a depreciating asset, and you want to have the least amount of your net worth in a depreciating asset while you are working on repairing and building your financial life. Of course, the transportation has to still reasonably accomplish its purpose, and I understand that not everyone wants to drive around in a car they find repulsive. You have to find a balance of what is best for your financial life and your happiness as you actually commute around in your vehicle.

I encourage you to focus on being smart when you make your next car purchase. Save enough of a down payment and be mindful when purchasing your next vehicle to be able to meet these guidelines at a bare minimum. Don't just focus on what looks nice or the luxury features the car has. Focus on getting a car that is safe, reliable, and falls into a budget that you can actually afford. If your current vehicle doesn't fit this category, then you may want to consider selling it and buying a car that does. Following these guidelines will help put you on the quickest path to financial success.

Your car can be one of the biggest things holding you back from building wealth, so treat this with as much seriousness as you would anything that is worth that much to your well-being. When you are looking for a car, don't just shop based on the monthly payment, because the dealer will extend your loan for years until it gets under that monthly amount. What you need to focus on is the final total purchase price that you will pay when you walk out the door—that final number on the bottom line, including all of the fees and extra charges. Focusing on this number will help prevent you from purchasing a car that brings about depreciation that is too big a percentage of your net worth.

Let's say that you are a thirty-year-old who is trying to get their feet under them, start their family, and has the average $55,000 income per year. You have $30,000 saved up in your retirement so far. If you go out and buy a $30,000 car, that is most of your net worth. You're trying to grow that net worth while you also have a depreciating asset just as large that's losing value constantly. It would be like driving your net worth away. Picture yourself tossing some of that net worth, which you worked so hard to build slowly, out the window every time you get in the car to go for a drive. You would be heavily counteracting what you are trying to accomplish. This is the time where you could smartly have around a $12,000 safe and reliable used car that you put a big enough down payment on to fall within those guidelines. That car will allow you to continue to build your net worth. As you continue to grow, each car that you buy can be a step up. Eventually, you will be in the position to be able to buy your dream car and barely even flinch at the price. But until then, let's focusing on actually building the wealth and not just trying to drive in a rich person's car.

Underwater

If you are driving a car that is a high portion of your net worth and want to look into selling it, you will be able to use what was going to car payments to increase the amount of income that you put toward paying down debts and building your own net worth. If you decide to become serious enough to sell your car in order to reap that benefit, then make sure you look at a private sale. That avenue will bring you much more money than a trade-in at the dealership. If your car is underwater, meaning that you wouldn't be able to make enough money to pay off the car by selling it, then you have to come up with the difference in cash to be able to fix that situation. It is still worth it to go ahead and sell the car because you stop the money bleed of depreciation as soon as you sign over the vehicle.

Overall, leasing a car is one of the most expensive ways to operate a vehicle over the long haul. Please do not do this if you are really focused on building wealth at this stage of your life. If you are at the end of your lease contract, you can simply choose to not renew and to buy yourself a vehicle to drive. If you are far enough from the end and need to get out of your lease contract, you may want to look into selling the car and paying off your early-buyout balance. Ensure you read your contract thoroughly as to not violate it in the process, but this goes to show that you are never too stuck in a lease to take back control of your financial life.

Pain Becomes Motivation

Downgrading cars will probably be one of the hardest decisions you make. It hurts to go from what you feel is something really nice to something less that is actually affordable for you. It hurts when people inevitably ask what happened to your nice car. Make sure you bottle that up as motivation and take pride in the fact that you are taking control of your finances. As people comment on your decision, just remind yourself that you are doing this now so that later you can drive even nicer cars when you will be in a much better position to be able to afford them.

Mortgage Refinance

If you own a home, a great place to look to save money is refinancing your mortgage. As of 2021, we have some of the lowest mortgage interest rates in history. This is a great time for those who bought their homes many years ago, when interest rates were higher, to go ahead and refinance to a much lower rate. By doing this, you will automatically lower your monthly payments. Ensure you look at the entire cost (fees and closing costs) of the refinance before making this decision. The money that you save from this can work wonders for your debt-elimination timeline.

Take Pride

Keep lifestyle deflation in mind every time you go shopping, get an offer, see an ad or sale, and so on. You should constantly be looking for ways to not pay as much as everyone else is paying. You'll know you've truly embodied this concept when you see a sale and still check online to see if you can beat it. When someone offers you a deal, the first thing that comes to mind will be whether you're getting the absolute best offer you can find. That's how you know you've mastered this thought process. It becomes a sense of pride and joy. When you find the best deal out there, you will be proud to say that you found something much cheaper than all your friends and be ecstatic. You will be happy to tell everyone and show them the retail price versus how much less you were able to get it for. It's a great feeling!

Lifestyle deflation has a lot in common with the frugality community. There is a whole foundation of people dedicated to finding the cheapest way to live the life they want to live. These people make videos, write articles, create web pages, and much more for us to learn from. They give you all the tools and resources that you need to figure out how to cut the price tag on your lifestyle down. If you need any extra resources, just look online and you will find more than enough.

Let Freedom Ring

Being free of crippling debt feels like breathing a breath of fresh air. Your financial stress and anxiety will be all but extinct, giving you so much more room to rest easy. You get to take pride in your journey to this stage and look at how far you have come while knowing this is just the beginning for you. This step is just one of the first major milestones I want you to experience. Hopefully you're excited to get here and feel the freedom of breaking away from the grip that debt has on us as consumers.

This point of being debt-free is where you can be even more motivational in helping others achieve the same. Finding and helping the average American with many debts and paying interest every month to someone else will be one of the most satisfying and fulfilling things you can do. Seeing that person gain control of their financial life and reach debt freedom is like seeing that person who works so hard in the gym later succeed in their sport, or flowers that you worked so hard to plant finally spring up and blossom. I encourage each person who has achieved debt freedom to reach out to at least one person and try to help them. You get to be an example of what they can do when they decide to take control of their life.

The Rich and Frugal

As you build your net worth later down the road, you will probably never fully lose this frugality mindset. You will always remember how much it accelerated your growth and won't want to go back to paying full price, retail, or an upcharge on anything that you buy. Some of the richest self-made millionaires in the world are some of the most frugal people that you will ever meet. There's a reason for that. They know it's what got them rich and will keep them rich. This is why they won't let the frugal mentality go, even when they have the money to do what they please. To put this in its most plain and simple terms, it is really just them being smart with their spending and putting efficiency first and foremost. Once you master lifestyle deflation in your own personal life, you will be well on your way to reaching your goals of getting those crippling debts paid off and beginning to build wealth.

PART 4: BUILDING

Savings: Part II

By this part of the journey, you should be free of all crippling debts in your life and confident in your budgeting and spending habits. It's really important that you now fully build up your cash pile to be an even better emergency safety net. Even if you have investments worth thousands, tens of thousands, or even hundreds of thousands of dollars, those investments will fluctuate up and down, causing this stable and liquid cash pile to be a necessary staple of your financial foundation. If you are in an emergency where you have to get your hands on cash, you don't want to be forced to sell your investments at a loss. It can take you days to turn it into cash on hand, but you need money that you can get your hands on almost instantly.

Think about where you'd be if you had $10,000 of your emergency fund in stock investments when we had a market downturn. Let's pretend it loses 40 percent of its value right at the moment when the economic slowdown also causes you to lose your job. Now you don't have $10,000 of cash savings anymore. You now only have a $6,000 fund, which may not be adequate anymore. Would you be able to afford to lose that much at the same time that you lost your income?

These are the types of situations that have happened and will continue to happen to unprepared people during market cycles. The whole point of investment planning is to ensure you are taking advantage of the economy in a smart and moral way during the good times while also maintaining a solid foundation to be ready to embrace the inevitable bad economic times. This is what makes having cash savings so important. The stability it brings you cannot be matched in the times you need it most. Even during the good times, knowing that you have protection helps you make more confident decisions to take the most advantage of opportunities while also being able to sleep well at night no matter the outcome.

Rule of Thumb

You should keep about three to six months' worth of cash that you can easily get your hands on. This gives you a wide window to decipher what is applicable to you. Where you fall on that scale will depend on what your stability levels are. If you work a job that you feel very comfortable in—you have been there for many years, the company is in great shape, and you don't have any pending financial burdens that you foresee—then you may be comfortable on the three-months'-worth-of-savings side of that scale. If this doesn't describe your situation, then you will move closer and closer to the six-months side of it. The scale is best judged by you because you know your situation better than anyone else.

What Counts

Three to six months of expenses means your necessities need to be covered: your mortgage, utilities, groceries, gas money, car insurance, and things of that nature. Keep in mind any contracts you owe on that will include hefty late fees or penalties. If failure to pay a bill on a service contract at your business will rack up hundreds of dollars in late fees, this may then need to be included in your emergency fund amount because preventing this damage becomes a necessity. You can exclude anything that wouldn't hurt you financially to give up in an emergency. Things like dining out allotments, subscriptions, spending-money allocations, and so on do not need to be counted.

Having this savings cushion fully stocked will give you the needed confidence to fill your life with financial stability and peace. If you have healthy savings set aside and something happened at your job, it gives you time to adjust to your situation and make more rational choices about how to move forward. It won't take away all of the stress of an emergent situation by any means, but the stress would be manageable because you won't instantly be on the verge of bankruptcy. You know that your expenses will be covered while you're working through that tough period in your life. It will keep you from having to do anything desperate, and we all know that desperation leads to bad financial decisions.

Where to Stash

Once you have a fully funded cash stockpile, your savings from there will be for short-term things, like saving for a vacation or Christmas presents. All things of this nature are too short-term to be worth it to invest that money. These types of things are best done in a separate account away from your emergency savings to segment your accounts. You generally want to avoid mixing these two together because it may tempt you to dip into your emergency-fund savings to cover your vacation or Christmas with the expectation that you will pay it back later. Don't put yourself in that tempting position; just keep your savings accounts separate for the most protection.

It feels like your money should be working for you rather than sitting there potentially for a few years, so the logical question would be where exactly to put this money to get the most benefit from your savings. It's easily accessible for most people to open new savings accounts for free, so you can take advantage of that feature where you can find it. But with interest rates being so low in our current economy, there are a few options to give you a better rate of return.

A high-yield savings account with an FDIC-insured bank will provide a better rate of return. Your money will meet the requirements for safety and liquidity while also beating interest rates on the average savings account. Usually, online savings banks can offer the most competitive rates of return because of the low overhead costs associated with moving away from the classic brick-and-mortar banking institutions.

For the purposes of safe savings vehicles, a money market account is also comparable to a high-yield savings account. You won't go wrong with either choice, so make your decisions based on your level of comfort with the bank and the fee structures and stipulations on the specific accounts. In an environment where interest rates increase, your choice of savings vehicle may need to be reevaluated.

You will want to avoid using a certificate of deposit (CD) for your emergency savings unless you understand and accept the early-withdrawal penalties associated with your specific certificate. This will help avoid any unexpected surprise fees should you need to access your cash. However, a CD can be a great tool to use for other short-term savings goals with a timeline for when you know you will need the money. For example, if you plan to buy a house when you move in eighteen months, then a CD may be a great tool for you to use. It will provide you a much better rate of return than a savings account while also allowing you to avoid the risk of an untimely downturn in the market when you need the cash. It will also prevent you from using the money earlier for anything else without penalty while it is supposed to be waiting for your pending move. A CD can be a great tool for savings in this current low-interest-rate environment if the structure and terms of your specific CD are well understood beforehand.

Investing

Every topic so far has been all about getting you to a place where you have a plan and a sound financial foundation. You should be confident in where you are now and headed into the future. I'm confident that you feel protected and at peace in your financial life because you don't have any outstanding consumer debts and are completely owning your lifestyle. Now let's get ready to start focusing your attention on investing in the future that you want to build for yourself. Why do we want you to invest in your future? We want you to invest because this is a chance for you to start building a portfolio of assets that will begin working for you.

The point of investing is to reverse the fact that you spend so much time working for someone else to make money to live on. Now it's time for you to put your money to work for you so that you will eventually not have to work as hard for your income. We are talking about reaching financial freedom here. Investing is just the medium that we use to help us get there.

Investing may sound scary. It may sound like you are putting your money at risk of loss; however, learning how to invest is all about minimizing the risk. Educating yourself before making investment decisions will remove the sense of gambling away your money and make you confident in your strategy. Just ask yourself: Do you think that the millionaires and billionaires of the world have their net worth in investments that they feel are gambling? The answer is that they do not. They are very confident in their financial futures because they are educated enough in investing to make strategic investment decisions based on data, history, and realistic future outlooks. The challenge to you now is to get educated enough on investments to make confident and informed decisions as well. The resources are all out there on the internet. Between free videos, articles, and podcasts, you can learn enough to get started. Financial professionals are also here to help get you started and to give you an expert opinion.

Risk Is Always Present

Let's start with a thought experiment to put investment risks into perspective. Money that you have is always at risk of a loss. Cash stored in your house would be at risk of theft. It would also be consistently at a loss due to inflation over time. You could minimize the risk of theft by putting your money in the bank. The bank pays almost no interest on that money, so it is still guaranteed to make a small, consistent loss due to inflation over time. On the opposite side of the spectrum, you could invest in a high-risk loan to a private individual and run the risk of losing all your money in a bad deal. Hopefully, this spectrum shows you that we are always running some type of risk with our money. You may wonder what to do with your money if you are constantly running some level of risk. The answer is to find your balance of investing by educating yourself and determining what a good investment is for you. It should always be one that makes you comfortable with the level of risk associated with it. As you get into that investment, use your knowledge to best minimize whatever risk there is. Since it's impossible to avoid risks with money, you should always have a well-thought-out plan that you are following and that allows you to enjoy the journey and results.

The List Never Ends

Let's talk about what investments are out there. It would be impossible for us to cover every single type of investment there is. We'll just cover some common ones to give you enough to know where to begin looking. You have low-risk investments, such as US Treasury notes, government bonds, municipal bonds, and so on. You have predictably volatile investments, such as many stock market equities. You have high-overhead investments, such as real estate deals. You have sweat-equity investments, such as running your own business as a hands-on owner. You have high-risk and high-reward investments, such as private lending. The list goes on and on. There are almost endless investments that you can get into. The key is that getting out of debt and building money to invest with gives you the opportunity to take those investments while minimizing the risks to your financial lifestyle.

Build It Yourself

One of the most practical investment solutions for those with a skill or expertise is to start their own business taking advantage of their skill. A professional carpenter may launch a business taking on carpentry subcontracts. A doctor may go out and start their own clinic. A cook or chef may open their own restaurant. These professionals already know the skill and intricacies of their field, so they can be great candidates for starting a successful business. The knowledge from years of experience in the industry makes the risks of starting the business much more comfortable. This is a prime example of how education and experience reduce investment risks, which increase the odds of finding success. It takes so much dedication to saving and building your financial foundation to even be ready and able to make an investment like this, so enjoy the opportunities that being in this position gives you.

Where to Start

You may be wondering where to get started investing. The answer is simple and complex at the same time. You want to ensure that you put yourself in the best position to be a prudent and successful investor. Your monthly expenses should be low and without excess payments on consumer goods like cars, furniture, and so on. You should have no outstanding credit card debts, medical bills, personal loans, or other crippling obligations. Ensure that the extra income you have is yours to do with as you please. This is the very first step toward protecting yourself against the worst outcomes of unsuccessful investments.

The next step is to educate yourself on what it is you want to invest in. Let's say you want to get started in real estate. Learn the ins and outs of the real estate industry and local market where you want to invest. Try to find someone in the field that you can talk to about it. You should read so many articles and books and watch so many videos that it becomes hard to find new, pertinent information on your intended sector. As soon as you objectively feel comfortable with your level of knowledge, then you can carefully move into the investment.

If you decide on a high-overhead investment such as real estate or a trucking business, then something else to consider is funding. You may know the game of truck driving and how the business works; buying your own truck or trucks, however, can still be a daunting task. Funding can happen in so many different ways. As a general rule, remember to objectively consider how much debt you take on to get started in your business. You never want to be in over your head with so much debt that you would be absolutely crushed financially in the event of a business failure.

Those who can't immediately monetize their current career into their own business can always learn a new trade, skill, or industry to get started in something fresh. Think about something that you would enjoy. Look up the entry requirements and get started. Don't let the requirements scare you away from something that you feel would be an answer to your dreams. Just take everything one step at a time. If it requires a license, then look at getting a license as one step to complete. If it requires a certain application to regulators, then look at learning regulations and getting approval as just one step. The key is to just get started without mentally blocking yourself from ever taking the first steps toward your dream.

Choose Your Style

There are two general types of investing: active and passive. Active investing means that you are diligently extending your time and your knowledge in that investment in order to earn an income. Active investments can usually give you the highest payoff in the long run. It could be opening a business with yourself on the front lines answering calls, opening doors, and doing the work in that business to make it run. You are investing your time and resources along with your money in active investments.

In passive investments, you place your money into the deal, business, or equity in hope of letting it work for you mostly in your absence. The investments are usually either risky with a possibility for high returns or low risk with likely low returns. These investments generally have a much lower return rate than active investments. Which type is best for you will depend on what you find fits your situation and level of desired involvement in the investment.

An example of passive investing could be buying real estate with the intent to hire a property manager to handle the day-to-day functions of running the property. A more common example would be investing in the stock market. These are all passive investments because you put little to no time into getting your return on your investment. You don't need years of experience in a skill to do passive investing, which appeals to a lot of investors.

Passive investing can also be a tool used to begin while you are preparing to take on another more active investment. It is very logical to invest in the stock market for a few years while you are working through building enough experience and knowledge of another industry that you plan to invest in later.

Whichever way you choose to invest, be it actively, passively, or some combination of both, there is something out there for everyone. Once you start taking ownership of income-producing assets or businesses, then you begin to accelerate your wealth building. The biggest benefit is that you can begin getting out of the cycle of earning your income only by trading time that could be spent better with family and friends or doing something that you truly enjoy and are fulfilled by.

The Farmer

A great illustration is the fable of the farmer who cuts down trees in his forest every summer to prepare firewood for the winter. While other farmers were harvesting crops and cutting just enough wood to get by, this farmer worked very hard to harvest and cut enough wood to ensure his family had excess for even the worst of winters. He cut and harvested so much that he eventually had enough supplies to last more than four consecutive winters. People told him he had so much that he wouldn't have to harvest or cut for years.

As you can imagine, this was a great place to be, but he had other plans in mind for all his hard work. He saw that he had enough excess wood to build two cabins. He also sold enough supplies to buy enough land to support the two cabins. He built them and sold them to two families. One family had a deal to have the cabin and land in exchange for providing enough wood to maintain the farmer's heat throughout the winters. The other family had a deal to have the other cabin and land in exchange for harvesting enough crops for his family to eat throughout the year. The farmer never again was forced to trade his physical labor for firewood and food for his family for the rest of their lives. He instead chose to spend his time farming and cutting wood leisurely to buy more land and build more cabins at whatever pace he chose to continue building the legacy for his children.

We are farmers working hard to make ends meet year after year. We can choose to work hard and smart enough to create excess money in our lives. We can then take that money and invest it into building something that will support us and help end the cycle of being forced to trade our time for our money. The formula is there and has been proven time and time again.

Manage, Not Avoid

For those of you who are hesitant to invest money because you aren't convinced that the name of the game is managing risk, not avoiding it altogether, let's think about how business owners view risk. An owner of a company at some point put their money and credit on the line to start their business. They saw an opportunity to monetize their skills and took it. There is obviously risk in this with every business because owners are always dependent on the customer buying their product or services to keep them afloat. However, they are so confident that they have effectively managed the risks with the income potential that they are willing to hire you at a promised salary for years. By doing that, they are accepting that there may be downtimes in the business when they still have to pay you a salary—they would have to live with the consequences. But they are also only obligated to pay you what they promised upon hiring, even during the times that business is booming.

The owners and managers obviously see more value in hiring you than they do risks of negative outcomes to their business model. They identified the risks, weighed them, and went forward in investing in hiring you in the face of the many potential risks. They run the risk of the business failing and still being forced to pay you, or hiring a terrible worker that could cost the company money in losses or lawsuits from customers. They run a lot of risk by hiring you, yet companies hire all the time. They understand that the process is all about risk management, not complete avoidance.

Not to say that everyone should go out and start their own business, but it's very important to understand the difference in how successful business owners view opportunities and risks. Their minds work toward how to best learn about, manage, and minimize risks—not trying to avoid them at all costs. That's what gets them to the point of being the smart financial decision makers that we view them as. We can take a step toward being as smart as them by learning to view every opportunity through the lens of wanting to objectively learn about the risks and how to mitigate them rather than avoiding learning of the unknown when any risk is present.

Like we said before, the name of the game is risk management, not avoiding any risk at all costs. That is because the truth is that we can't avoid risk in our financial lives. We learned that even the money you stashed away at an FDIC-insured bank is at risk. That risk is an almost-guaranteed slow leak in practical value due to inflation. You've worked hard to get to the point of creating excess income, so let's continue our education in investing and risk management to ensure we can be smart, effective managers of our own wealth.

Retirement Investing

You should already be taking advantage of your retirement-account matching contributions from your employer if this incentive is available at your job. Retirement investing from there can take on many forms that all depend on how you intend to design your retirement lifestyle. A great rule of thumb is to invest at least 15 percent of your gross income for retirement. This rule helps set the floor for you to hopefully have a healthy sum of money to supply your income when you no longer desire to work as much or as hard.

Take the time to learn your avenues available to take advantage of some of the tax-incentivized forms of investing for retirement first. This will help you maximize your contributions by saving you tax dollars either now or in the future. With the hope of encouraging you to start reserving at least 15 percent of your income for retirement, let's talk about some of the common retirement vehicles available to save and invest through.

401(k)

For those with a 401(k) from their employer, you can make further contributions past your matching limit to this account for your retirement investing. This is a great tool to use because it allows you to easily take advantage of tax benefits provided by our government under the protection of not directly seeing the contributions or balance on a regular basis, which also helps prevent it from tempting you to tap into it too early. It's one of the most common vehicles used to build and protect wealth, so there's some credibility to its usage.

A traditional 401(k) provides you with tax-deferred savings. This means that you do not pay income taxes on your contributions when you fund the account. Those taxes will not be due until you withdraw the money in your retirement. For those who foresee a lower-tax environment for themselves in the future, this can be a great tool to save money in the present that can be used to help you make bigger contributions and grow your account faster. The disclaimer here is that you may be doing yourself a disservice by not at least considering the present tax savings as an opportunity to fund the account more. Seeing this savings as free spending money would not be taking full advantage of the tax incentive to help prepare you better for the future.

A Roth 401(k) is another type of 401(k) that comes with a different form of tax advantages. In this account you are taxed in the present on the money when you fund your account; however, you will not pay income taxes when you make withdrawals in your retirement from the basis or gains. This can be a great tool for those who are not presently in a high tax bracket and see benefit in paying their taxes upon funding the account to allow for future tax-free growth.

IRA

An IRA, like a 401(k), is a tax-advantaged retirement account designed to help fund a financially healthy retirement. This account is not employer sponsored and can be opened through a brokerage firm for personal or professional management. It can be created as a traditional tax-deferred account that is tax deductible in the present, or you can choose a Roth account that provides tax-free income in the future.

These are some of the most common accounts that people should take advantage of when investing for retirement. The tax treatment has the potential to save a great deal of money in the future for those using them. Other tax-advantaged accounts may fit well into how you want to design your financial future, so it's important to take the time to do your research or seek financial counsel to ensure you're making decisions that get you closer to your goals most efficiently.

Key Points

Remember that just putting money in the account isn't enough. You have to tell the money in the account how you want it to work for you. This is where diligent research, or an investment adviser for larger estates, can help put you on a path to success. A great baseline for retirement savings for individuals trying to figure out a place to begin can be low-cost target-date funds or index funds. These can give you a fantastic start, but remember that nothing can replace doing your own research to build your confidence and determine what is best for you. Once you begin building a significant net worth, the margin of efficiency that a financial professional can provide you will likely be a great investment. No matter where you are in your financial literacy currently, you will get the hang of it, develop a confident investing plan, carry it out, and watch your plan produce results.

Investing 15 percent of your gross income works as a rule of thumb to ensure you're not investing too little. Investing more than this into retirement accounts should be done with a plan that accommodates not wanting to access this money until after age 59½. Accessing your money before this age may come with penalties on earnings and income taxes on deferred accounts. Your plan may end up consisting of investing funds outside of tax-advantaged accounts to be able to access them without penalty before age 59½. The theme here is to ensure that what you do follows a plan that fits your situation and goals for your future.

The other key thing to remember is that deciding which type of account to focus your retirement savings on is not a mutually exclusive deal. You can, and I recommend that you do, use a mixture of different accounts to take a more full advantage of the savings provided by our tax code. This helps allow you to fit the funding limits of the accounts but also helps protect you from possible future tax-code changes that could affect the outcome of your years of planning. A healthy mixture of diversity in your plan usually always provides the best, safest result.

Big Picture

Part 4 of the journey is where your wealth building really begins. By continuing to use the financial documents in your tool belt, you will have a plan for your savings and investing goals that fits well into your financial picture. I encourage you to develop a system around meeting these goals to allow your wealth to build almost as if being done in the background. Set your recurring contributions to automatically fund your respective accounts. Investment accounts can be set to invest automatically within the account as well. Once your system is put into motion, all you have to do is refrain from interrupting it. Make periodic financial wellness checks when you update your documents or make updates to your system, but your accounts should be largely left undisturbed to build. This helps reduce the emotional factor of building wealth that can cause the type of stress that often leads to mistakes. Allow yourself the mental freedom of knowing that you have a system in place working around the clock for you. By automating our system, we spend less time actively thinking about managing our money and simultaneously making it difficult to fail to meet our goals. This takes a lot of the pressure and angst of personal finance away as your wealth begins to grow.

PART 5: LIVING

The typical person that goes through all the steps of paying off their debts, building healthy savings, and beginning to invest in assets gets to the point where they are finally able to see their portfolio and net worth start to grow and work for them. The biggest source of struggle at this point is relearning how to enjoy spending their money. It is almost ironic that spending money is the difficulty people have after becoming debt-free and thinking like an investor.

Spending so much time being frugal and practicing lifestyle deflation usually means that retaining all your money and living only on minimal expenses becomes the norm. It's so satisfying to see the growth and feel the accomplishment that it almost doesn't feel right to go out on vacation or have a really nice, expensive dinner because everything feels like a loss of opportunity. It almost becomes a guilty feeling. It's time to liberate yourself from some of the constraints that you put on your money to get to this point. Let's talk about how we do that.

There are indicators that it's okay to take your foot off the gas pedal: you are investing enough that you feel confident your retirement needs will be satisfied, and you are on track for building assets to meet any other goals you've set. After these two conditions are met, you should relax some of the constraints that you put on your money up to this point. This is all assuming that you have constructed reasonable goals and expectations for your retirement based upon data and history. There is no perfect science here, so the best you can do is be realistic and conservative on the math.

Everything outside of these two requirements should be looked at as money that needs to be proportioned. You can proportion money toward anything that you want to save for, invest with, or spend on; however, you should always proportion some for enjoyment. Maybe you decide that out of $1,900 left over after all bills, retirement contributions, and savings goals are met, you will set aside $1,200 toward free spending money. You should feel free to enjoy that money that you chose to set aside specifically for this purpose. Don't feel guilty about spending a few hundred on a nice night out if it's not being funded by debt, the spending fits inside of your enjoyment category in your budget, and you have fully funded all your other savings and investment goals first. This is how you truly have an enjoyable and fulfilling time spending your money. This is your permission to now be able to buy a new outfit, order a limousine ride, have the finest dining experience in town, go on your dream vacation, make a generous donation to your favorite charity, buy the car you've always wanted, build your dream home, or do whatever it is that you've always wanted to do with your money. Feel free to live your best life. Let's just ensure you're meeting the criteria so your spending is done wisely.

If you are having trouble deciding the proportions you should set to enjoy, reach out to an unbiased third party that is equally or more financially acute. You can always consult a financial planner to help ensure you continue making smart money decisions. Either way you go about it, it's always beneficial to have someone unbiased in your life to weigh thoughts with to make sure that your spending stays under control.

It may be hard to believe that learning to spend your money can be the tough part of this process. At this step, however, this is a very common experience because you went through so much to get to where you are. You had to retrain your brain to think about having and using money differently. The fact that the focus is now on learning to enjoy spending money, instead of trying to save and invest every dime you get, is a testament to just how far you've come. Hopefully, this can be an easy and enjoyable transition period for you.

Again, we want to remind you to give back the knowledge you've learned. This step in the journey presents another great opportunity to do that. Hopefully, you are seeking others to help along this process to make sure they are making wise financial decisions that set them up for future success. Be the teacher, example, and motivation that someone else needs.

Legacy Planning

If you were to try to compare how finances fit into your overall life, it would be like a puzzle made up of a ton of little pieces that all fit together differently for everyone. One of the last big puzzle pieces would be legacy planning. This piece can be extremely complex and should not be taken lightly once your finances are as advanced as to have completed all the steps of the book thus far.

For most people, legacy plans never really become a big focus until it's too late. It ends up being your heirs that will have to bear the burden of any lack of planning in this field. If you care about your dependents or heirs, you will want to leave a legacy plan to help them financially and to smooth out foreseen issues as best as you can in the event of your loss. This will also alleviate some of the stress that comes with losing a loved one and help allow them time for proper mourning. Let's briefly talk about the why and how behind some of the aspects of legacy planning to ensure you understand why this piece is so important.

Consequences

Let's put this into perspective. We're going to take a married couple with children that had no life insurance, will, or legacy plan in place. If a spouse were to pass away, they would likely leave a large financial burden on their family as they try to deal with the loss of a loved one and care for the family, children, and finances. That's why it's important to have life insurance as part of your legacy plan if financial trouble would ensue.

If both parents were to pass, their kids would go through a long court process with the state deciding who will receive custody of the children. The parents may have verbally said they would want their brother, sister, parents, or a family friend to take care of the children in the event of their loss, but these plans have to be in writing and filed properly. Otherwise, the court will take over care for the children until they find what they deem is a responsible party best suited to give them a home. Anyone feeling they should be the guardian would be able to try to convince the state, through the court system, that they are in fact the right fit for the children. The person you actually want caring for your children may now spend months in court trying to prove themselves the best fit before a permanent home for the children is finally decided. A simple way to avoid this issue would be leaving a legacy plan that tells the state exactly what you want to happen after your loss. This will save your children from any issues and confusion in court about who is the best fit for being their guardian. You will also save your future guardian the time, money, and heartache of going through this process. It is in everyone's best interest to think through things such as how you will provide financial support to the new guardian of your children. It would be detrimental if your loss caused your new guardian and children to be placed into financial ruin due to this lack of planning.

People often think about their will only when talking about legacy planning. However, things like filing guardianship provisions for your children and preparing the guardian financially are no less important than deciding how your assets will be handled. Make time to think through all aspects of your final wishes and get them filed properly. Your heirs and successor will greatly benefit from it.

Probate

Let's talk about what happens to the belongings in your estate, such as vehicles, a home, bank accounts, and so forth, when you die. Your estate will go through probate, a process where the court will decide how to best delegate your assets to your heirs. Anyone that thinks they may lay claim to anything that you owned in your estate will also freely be able to fight for your assets in court. This process can be lengthy and costly, so it's not something you will wish to put your family or friends through.

To simplify the probate process, you should have beneficiaries named for all your accounts, from bank accounts to retirement accounts, brokerage accounts, and any accounts that have value in them. Having beneficiaries for your accounts can help keep these assets from going through probate; they will instead pass directly to the designated heir. Any physical assets that you have, such as your cars and home, should be named to a beneficiary in a will to make the probate process as smooth as possible.

Trusts Are for Any of Us

If you desire an efficient legacy plan that will take care of your intended heirs during your estate's settlement while avoiding the complications of the probate process, then a trust may fill your needs. This is a tool that is underutilized by most Americans because of a lack of knowledge that things like this are available to them. Most people think that trusts are only for the ultrawealthy. That is false; everyone has access to create and use them to the full extent of the law, but people need to be told what is available to them in order to make use of their resources.

Think of a trust as a separate entity that you can create and pass the ownership of your assets to. A person of your choosing is designated to handle the trust and its assets upon your death. They will execute your wishes as laid out in your trust documents until all the wishes have been met and the assets have been delegated to the new owners. This process never triggers probate within the court system. It allows your estate to be settled with minimum headache to your beneficiaries and without their spending months in court advocating for your wishes during the probate process. This is a powerful tool for those in this stage of wealth building and goes unmatched at providing peace of mind for your loved ones. If this tool can provide the legacy you want to leave, talk with an estate attorney to learn more personalized advice about taking advantage of this underutilized instrument and get a trust set up for your loved ones.

Once you begin the process of legacy planning, you will be more at peace, knowing that your family and friends will be taken care of when you can no longer be present. What it takes to ensure this sense of security is much less than the mess that can unravel with no legacy plan in place. With that being said, because you love your loved ones, prepare to set them up for success. Hopefully this chapter convinced you that legacy planning looks different for everyone and can be extremely complex. I strongly encourage you to think these topics through and hire an estate attorney to guide your decisions and ensure they are put into place correctly. One of the only guarantees we have in life is that we will die someday, so let's leave behind a legacy that fulfills our journey.

JUST THE BEGINNING

After reading this book, you now know the steps to building a sound financial future. It all starts with knowledge, confidence, and motivation—the keys to getting started toward making progress. The goal of this book was to provide that foundation of knowledge needed for you to take the first steps and learn the basics behind how to get started building a more complete financial plan. Efficiency is key here, so seek help and guidance if any doubt or concerns arise.

Learning the knowledge doesn't go very far if it's never applied to your life. If this book motivated you to take action in any way, don't wait. Take the action now before you lose any focus or motivation. Go ahead and earmark or highlight the key points that you know you should be working on now to ensure you don't put them off any longer. Follow along the checklist to make sure you stay on track. Most of these actions cost you nothing more than some time and dedication, so don't let this opportunity to take advantage of your heightened motivation pass you by.

Implementing the lessons in this book will move you beyond the category of the 65 percent of Americans currently living paycheck to paycheck. We don't want you fumbling through your financial life and hoping that things will just simply hold together. Years of schooling didn't teach and prepare us well enough for this important aspect of our lives, and now we are left to figure it out. The playing field has been leveled, and you now have the knowledge to begin putting yourself on track to excel financially, no matter what opportunities were or were not granted for you to learn these principles from an early age. Take advantage of this knowledge and share it with others to lift us all toward more successful and less stressful financial lives.

"Honor the LORD with your wealth…"

--Proverbs 3:9

CPSIA information can be obtained
at www.ICGtesting.com
Printed in the USA
BVHW040845271221
624880BV00018B/1076

9 781638 372899